Reading Shaver's Creek

Reading
Shaver's
Creek

Ecological

Reflections

from an

Appalachian Forest

EDITED BY IAN MARSHALL

The Pennsylvania State University Press | University Park, Pennsylvania

KEYSTONE BOOKS

Keystone Books are intended to serve the citizens of Pennsylvania. They are accessible, well-researched explorations into the history, culture, society, and environment of the Keystone State as part of the Middle Atlantic region.

Library of Congress Cataloging-in-Publication Data

Names: Marshall, Ian, 1954- editor.
Title: Reading Shaver's Creek : ecological reflections from an Appalachian forest / edited by Ian Marshall.
Description: University Park, Pennsylvania : The Pennsylvania State University Press, [2018] | "Keystone books." | Includes bibliographical references and index.
Summary: "A collection of essays on nature observations at the Shaver's Creek Environmental Center, focusing on deepening the connection of personal and cultural meanings to a specific place through a process of sustained close attention."—Provided by publisher.
Identifiers: LCCN 2017041160 | ISBN 9780271080208 (pbk. : alk. paper)
Subjects: LCSH: Shaver's Creek Environmental Center—Literary collections. | Stone Valley Recreation Area (Pa.)—Literary collections. | Human ecology—Pennsylvania—Stone Valley Recreation Area—Literary collections. | Forests and forestry—Pennsylvania—Stone Valley Recreation Area—Literary collections. | Creative nonfiction, American—21st century. | American essays—21st century. | American poetry—21st century.
Classification: LCC GF504.P4 R43 2018 | DDC 304.209748/73—dc23
LC record available at https://lccn.loc.gov/2017041160

The Pennsylvania State University Press is a member of the Association of American University Presses.

It is the policy of The Pennsylvania State University Press to use acid-free paper. Publications on uncoated stock satisfy the minimum requirements of American National Standard for Information Sciences—Permanence of Paper for Printed Library Material, ANSI z39.48–1992.

All photographs by Steven Rubin, 2016: hardhack on stump in Shaver's Creek near Twin Bridges (p. 18); Shaver's Creek near the Rudy Sawmill site (p. 34); Virginia creeper on a fence post at the Chestnut Plantation (p. 50); the Dark Cliffy Spot (p. 66); November in the Bluebird Meadow: oriental bittersweet climbing a black walnut tree (p. 82); Lake Perez (p. 100); Stone Valley picnic area on the Lake Trail (p. 118); red-shouldered hawk looking out at the world (p. 138).

CONTENTS

ACKNOWLEDGMENTS

First and foremost, my deep appreciation and gratitude to the staff at Shaver's Creek Environmental Center—and not just for supporting the Ecological Reflections Project. Shaver's Creek is a place that makes a difference in people's lives—and in the world. When I first moved to the State College area and was looking for places to hike, the Environmental Center and the surrounding Stone Valley trails were among my first discoveries. Some of my kids' first "biophilia" moments happened in front of the raptor cages. When my son worked, several years later, as a volunteer at the Raptor Center, animal caretakers Jen Brackbill and Doug Steigerwalt (and the many interns they oversaw) were as wonderfully nurturing with my son as they are with the birds in their care. When I came back from a conference with the idea for this Ecological Reflections Project, director Mark McLaughlin was immediately supportive, and his enthusiasm got the project off the ground. Naturalist/philosopher/guru Doug Wentzel (I think that's his official job title—or is it program director?), educational operations manager Josh Potter, and assistant marketing director Justin Raymond got things organized, accompanied visiting writers on tours of the sites, taught us bird calls (they are all amazing birders!), took care of all the arrangements (and payment!) for the visiting writers, and ushered the writers' words from scribbled notebook pages to online entries. Thanks as well to Jerod Skebo, naturalist intern extraordinaire, whose exuberant passion for the natural world exemplifies what Shaver's Creek Environmental Center is all about. And thank you to the writers who lent their creativity and time to reflect on a place that they may not have known well at first, but who have now added several solid layers to the deep map of Shaver's Creek and Stone Valley.

Todd Davis's poem "Spring Melt" appeared in his collection *In the Kingdom of the Ditch*, published by Michigan State University Press in 2013. It is reproduced here with the permission of Michigan State University Press.

The map of Shaver's Creek and the Stone Valley trails (produced by Justin Raymond) and the essays and photos from the Shaver's Creek Long-Term Ecological Reflections Project are reproduced here with the permission of the Pennsylvania State University and Shaver's Creek Environmental Center. You can find more of the Ecological Reflections Project essays, poems, and photos on the "Creek Journals" page of the Shaver's Creek website.

Some of the essays included here previously appeared in *Shavings*, the Shaver's Creek Environmental Center newsletter: Mike Branch's "In Search of Signs" (as "Site 1—Twin Bridges: Reflections by Mike Branch") in the Summer 2014 issue (pages 3–4); Jacy Marshall-McKelvey's "Looking into the Past: The Rudy Sawmill" in the Winter/Spring 2015 issue (pages 4, 11); Julianne Lutz Warren's "Lake Perez: Reflections" (as "Site 6—Lake Perez: Reflections by Julianne Lutz Warren") in the Summer/Fall 2016 issue (pages 8–10); and Katie Fallon's "Almost Lost" (as "'Almost Lost': Site 3—The Chestnut Plantation") in the Winter/Spring 2017 issue (pages 5–6). Steven Rubin's photo of the Chestnut Plantation also appeared in the Winter/Spring 2017 issue (page 6).

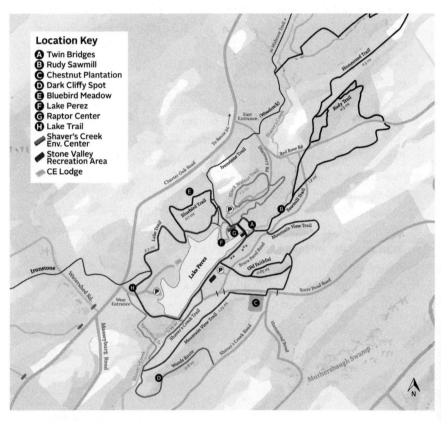

Shaver's Creek, Stone Valley trails, and the Ecological Reflections sites.
Map by Justin Raymond.

Introduction

Reading the Forested Landscape
Where to Begin

IAN MARSHALL

A blank page.

A forested landscape.

And the problem of how to put one onto another.

That was the task facing me back in 2006 when I ventured down to the "Twin Bridges," about a ten-minute walk down the Lake Trail from the Shaver's Creek Environmental Center in central Pennsylvania. The Twin Bridges reach across two branches of Shaver's Creek just about a hundred yards or so before the creek inlets into Lake Perez. There is a fortuitously placed sign there with the title "Reading the Shaver's Creek Landscape." It refers to Tom Wessels's classic text of environmental interpretation, *Reading the Forested Landscape*, and the sign points to various clues in the area that bespeak its history— evidence of beaver activity in downed and conically gnawed but still standing dead trees, a line of exposed hemlock roots indicating where a fallen "nurse log" once had lain, the open canopy above the stream where once it must have been beaver dammed. Okay, read the landscape, I told myself. I'm a literature professor—that's one thing I should know how to do: read things.

But where to begin? I had borrowed a GPS unit, so I took a reading. Data, I thought—that's what we should start with. Hard facts. Let's find out just where we are. Some numbers appeared on the screen, and I took out my brand-new notebook and wrote them down. Then the numbers changed, and changed again. But I hadn't moved, and while it's true that the creek was moving, it hadn't shifted its position on the planet. What was going on? One possibility was that it was not a very accurate GPS unit. Of course, the planet is in motion all the time, so maybe the changing figures on the screen were affected by that? And the satellites that were sending me the data—they were obviously in motion. And maybe the trees swaying in the spring wind interfered with the transmission between satellite and GPS unit?

It was lesson one. It's not so easy to know just where you are in the world. The place is changing all the time, always in motion. Data change. Yes, even facts as well as our perceptions are subject to change.

What does it mean to know a place? What can different academic disciplines teach us about the natural world? What might we learn about the world by returning to the same place year after year for, say, a hundred years? What would a long-term record of such visits tell us about change and permanence and our place in the natural world?

These are some of the questions explored by the Long-Term Ecological Reflections Project at Penn State University's Shaver's Creek Environmental Center and Stone Valley Experimental Forest. Each year, both a visiting nature writer and a Penn State faculty member who studies the natural world from the perspective of his or her own academic discipline visit eight designated sites in Stone Valley. At each site, the writer and scholar record what they see, their observations informed by their academic background or unique creative approach. A mammalogist might evaluate the site as habitat, while a poet may write a haiku. An environmental historian might seek clues as to past human habitation of the area, while a botanist could describe the plant life. For the creative nature writer, the topic of reflection might be a comparison of eastern forest and western desert, or the changes in a familiar landscape wrought by climate change. The essays included here constitute a "best of"—or at least a "representative of"—collection from the first decade of a hundred-year venture initiated in 2006.

The Ecological Reflections Project posits that knowledge of a place is the result of informed seeing from a number of different angles, and that both place itself and our knowledge and perceptions of it change over time. In addition to the long-term changes that are traced over the course of the next century, some respondents also track seasonal changes by spacing out their observations over the year. Visiting writers who are not able to make quick day trips out to Shaver's Creek over the course of a year stay for a week in one of the cabins at Stone Valley Recreation Area. The eight sites designated for study include the Twin Bridges area, the site of an old sawmill, an experimental chestnut orchard, the so-called Dark Cliffy Spot along an unnamed tributary of Shaver's Creek, the high point of the Bluebird Trail, and the raptor cages located behind the Environmental Center. Respondents also write about a circuit hike on the Lake Trail and about Lake Perez itself, the dominant landscape feature of the Stone Valley Recreation Area and Stone Valley Forest.

But talk about how quickly things can change. Remember the evidence of beaver activity I saw at Twin Bridges—the girdled trunks of dead hemlocks, the open canopy above the creek where all the trees had drowned and died off? There had been a pond there once, behind a beaver dam, and now it was gone. Presumably, the beaver dam was breached by wind, water, and entropy a season or two after the beavers left. And Lake Perez, its seventy-two-acre surface reposing behind the concrete dam constructed in 1960 by the beavers' mammalian relatives, has done its own disappearing trick. When the Ecological Reflections Project was started a dozen years ago, Lake Perez was there, and then a year later it was gone, emptied so that leaks in the dam could be repaired, which took seven years as funding issues caused delays. What was left was a winding stream through a muddy wetland. And now, as of a couple years ago, presto change-o, in the blink of a geological eye, the dam is back and there's a lake again.

The Ecological Reflections Project has its origins in a scholarly conference I attended in 2005, where I heard a presentation on Oregon State University's reflections project at H. J. Andrews Experimental Forest. Since 1980, the Andrews Forest has been one of twenty-eight sites in the National Science Foundation's Long-Term Ecological Research Network, and researchers there have studied such topics as the ecological role of the spotted owl in old-growth forests. But in the early years of the twenty-first century, a group of researchers, including stream ecologist Jim Sedell and environmental philosopher Kathleen Dean Moore, saw an opportunity to expand the inquiry beyond the natural sciences, and so in 2003 they started their ecological reflections project—"a humanities analog to the scientific research"—under the aegis of the Spring Creek Project for Ideas, Nature, and the Written Word at Oregon State University. It was Charles Goodrich, director of the Spring Creek Project, Fred Swanson, a senior fellow with Spring Creek, and Kathleen Dean Moore whom I had seen at that conference a decade or so ago.

At the Andrews Forest, the ecological reflectors visit four sites—a gravel bar, the "log decomposition plot," a recent clear-cut, and a selective-logging plot. According to Goodrich, the project encourages writers from the humanities to explore the "emotional and cultural relationships that humans have with both wild and managed landscapes," pointing out that scientific information on its own is rarely sufficient to sway public opinion and affect policy. The Andrews Forest Long-Term Ecological Reflections Project has compiled its own "best of" collection from its first dozen or so years, gathered in the cleverly titled *Forest Under Story*. In the introduction, Goodrich notes that "the causes of habitat degradation reside in the stories people tell themselves . . . about their relationships with other creatures, with the processes of nature, and with the land." In exploring those relationships, the writers are engaged in an act that is both restoration and "re-story-ation."[1]

After first hearing about the Andrews project at that conference thirteen years ago, I returned home to State College excited about the idea of ecological reflecting, and the next day made my weekly visit to Shaver's Creek. When I moved to the area more than a quarter century ago, Shaver's Creek was one of the first places I discovered for hiking and cross-country skiing, and when my kids were young it was a frequent destination, mainly so the kids could look at the hawks, eagles, vultures, and owls at the Raptor Center, and at the snakes and turtles inside the Environmental Center building. One of my earliest recognitions of my four-year-old son's precocious reading ability came when he read the words "northern harrier" off a sign in front of one of the raptor cages. I remember Corky Potter, founder of the Environmental Center, kindly explaining to my kids why leaves of deciduous trees might be bigger on the lower branches, as they strive to absorb the little sunlight that makes it through the upper canopy. My kids eventually went to summer camps at Shaver's Creek, and at the time when I was returning from that conference in 2005, my homeschooled son was working as a volunteer at the Raptor Center. Every Monday afternoon he would sweep out eagle cages, put out food (mostly dead mice) for the birds, and take turtles for a walk on the front lawn of the center while I took a hike around the lake.

On that particular day thirteen years ago, I returned from my hike and told Mark McLaughlin, director of Shaver's Creek, about the Andrews Forest project, and Mark immediately suggested that we could do something similar at Shaver's Creek, combining opportunities for environmental research with creative expression on behalf of a beloved landscape. We started slowly, with me volunteering to do a pilot set of writings and establish the sites, aiming for diversity of forest types and habitat. Over the years, funding support for the initiative has grown, and we've managed to put together an impressive roster of contributors.

The Shaver's Creek version of the Long-Term Ecological Reflections Project borrows many elements from the original project in the Andrews Experimental Forest: writers visit designated sites in the forest, meditate on what they see, and write about the experience. And we certainly share the impulse to "restory" the forest. But there are a few key differences. At the Shaver's Creek version, we have sought to include a healthy dose of local voices—and of course we have different sorts of sites, reflecting the different geography, climate, and land-use history of our area. And since at Shaver's Creek there was not already an ongoing research project approaching the landscape from the perspective of the natural sciences, we are eager to include the voices of scientists in our reflections—with biologists Carolyn Mahan and Julianne Lutz Warren being the first of what we hope will be many representatives from the natural sciences to share their perspectives.

So that's the history of the project. The question in terms of the scholarly context is why there is so much excitement over such ventures now. It's not as though this is an entirely new idea: Henry Thoreau was doing something like an ecological reflection in place with his decade-long Kalendar project of the 1850s, where he painstakingly recorded, month by month and year by year, the dates and details of annual events (the ice breakup on the river, the first robin's appearance, the first buds on the huckleberry bushes, the first berries). But perhaps Thoreau's project also holds the answer: at the time, nobody paid any attention to his project. It wasn't published in his lifetime, and none of his neighbors quite understood what he was up to. In recent years, however, not only has a new generation of literary critics gotten excited about this wealth of newly published Thoreauviana; so have scientists. Ecologist Richard Primack, in *Walden Warming: Climate Change Comes to Thoreau's Woods* (2014), has turned to Thoreau's meticulous records in order to track the effects of climate change as it has in turn affected the timing of seasonal change in Massachusetts. It has become apparent that paying attention to changes in a landscape over time has value—sometimes value that we are not even aware of at the moment of recording what we can see.

And that awareness about the importance of paying attention to the places we value is tied in with a series of other developments in the scholarly world. Perhaps because of our heightened and newly acute concerns over human impacts on planetary systems, the past couple of decades have seen a flourishing of programs in environmental studies and environmental science. In the ecological sciences there has been deepening concern about biodiversity loss—in terms of both species and habitats. Across several disciplines there has been a movement in just the past few years to label the new geological epoch the "Anthropocene," reflecting the sense that in our time human impact has become the most dominant force affecting planetary systems. The humanities have seen the rise of "ecocriticism" (ecologically oriented literary criticism) and the burgeoning of scholarly journals dedicated to it, as well as an ever-growing international scholarly organization dedicated to interdisciplinary literary studies, the Association for the Study of Literature and Environment. Twenty years ago the very term "ecocriticism" was met with bewilderment and raised eyebrows—and with mockery about tree huggers reading books made from dead trees. Now it requires neither explanation nor defense.

Perhaps these ecological reflections will be of particular interest to practitioners of "geocriticism," an offshoot of ecocriticism with origins in the writings of French critic Bertrand Westphal. The "central tenets" of geocriticism, according to Eric Prieto, neatly match the goals of this Ecological Reflections Project. Prieto explains that geocriticism is "geocentric," meaning that place, rather than author or genre or text, is its main subject. The point of a geocritical analysis is to "look at as many textual representations of [a] place as possible" in order to facilitate a "better understanding of the place," as opposed to a better understanding of an author or text. Second, geocriticism is "multifocal," or polyphonic, meaning that the idea is to gather many different perspectives on a place. Next, a geocritical analysis is "stratigraphic," or as Westphal himself puts it, the emphasis is on "spatiotemporality," as the examination of place must consider how it changes over time. Finally, geocriticism is "polysensorial," trying to get beyond the "visual bias" we usually bring to descriptions of place, calling attention to the textures, smells, and sounds of place. Overall, says Prieto, the goal "is to pick a place and study it from every conceivable angle: over time, across cultures, using multiple senses, and without prioritizing any single perspective."[2] That sounds a lot like what we are up to in this project, offering multiple perspectives over time as many writers look at the same place. Several of the writers collected here seem particularly fascinated by the temporal layers they perceive in the sites they visit, as in Scott Weidensaul's envisioning of the workings of the old Rudy Sawmill, and several are particularly sensitive to the ways in which the sites touch their senses beyond the visual, as in Mike Branch's delight in the creek music at the Dark Cliffy Spot.

Of course, it is not just scholars who have been part of this explosion of interest in what is sometimes called "place studies." We are in a golden age of nature writing. Think of how many of our most admired and honored contemporary writers have worked extensively in the genre: Peter Matthiessen, John McPhee, David Quammen, Terry Tempest Williams, Annie Dillard, Barry Lopez, Wendell Berry (this could be a very long list, so I'll stop here). Closer to home here in central Pennsylvania, we have our own local treasure in Marcia Bonta, author of nine books, four of which track the changes in her home landscape on Brush Mountain (outside Tyrone) through the seasons: *Appalachian Spring*, *Appalachian Summer*, *Appalachian Autumn*, and (you guessed it) *Appalachian Winter*.

I won't belabor the point further, but I will try to sum it up concisely: more than ever before, it seems, perhaps because of the ever-intensifying causes for environmental concern, writers and scholars are paying attention to changes in the land. The contributors collected herein are an impressive bunch, with almost a hundred book publications (and counting!) between them. Local writers and artists contributing to the Ecological Reflections Project in the first ten years, in addition to Marcia Bonta, are photographer Steven Rubin, poet Todd Davis, biologist Carolyn Mahan, and Shaver's Creek interns Hannah Inglesby and Jacy Marshall-McKelvey. Also from Pennsylvania is Scott Weidensaul, a Pulitzer Prize finalist in 2000 for his book *Living on the Wind*. Ecologist Julianne Lutz Warren lives in neighboring New York, and nature writer Katie Fallon lives in another neighboring state, West Virginia. Others have come from farther afield: writer and ecocritic Mike Branch from Nevada, nature writers David Gessner and John Lane from South Carolina, and poet David Taylor from Texas (by way of New York).

Besides offering a collection of place-based nature writing, the Ecological Reflections Project is also a research venture that involves tracing changes in the landscape. One of the intriguing prospects of the project is that we actually do not know what the long-term benefits of the project might be in the future—just as Henry Thoreau would have had no idea a century and a half ago that his observations of the environs around Concord, Massachusetts, would one day serve as crucial evidence in tracking the effects of climate change. But here's what we do know: the accumulating testimonies of the Ecological Reflections Project will provide an ongoing record of what one particular central Pennsylvania ecosystem, in Stone Valley, looks like through the twenty-first century. We know that the land and the creatures that dwell thereon are bound to change: the Ecological Reflections Project will track and record the nature of that change, giving us a time-lapse view of the unfolding ecological character of the Shaver's Creek landscape.

The ecological dimension of the project is especially evident in the more naturalist-oriented essays collected here, where we learn which birds were calling at a particular time and place—and what their calls sound like. We learn the names of flowers and trees, and how the settlement history in this valley was shaped by the local environment in the past—and how the environment was in turn shaped by human activity. All of that factual sort of information contributes to a mosaic of thoughtful naturalists' encounters with the landscape. But not all the nature writers collected here would consider themselves expert naturalists, and from the nonexperts we get, rather than a record of natural facts, a record of sensibilities at work pondering the cultural, spiritual, and psychological implications of changes in the landscapes we cherish. And from all the nature writers here, biologists and poets alike, we find an indication of the environmental concerns of our time and place—so you'll see a great deal of concern about topics like forest succession and alien species. What will be mapped over time, then, are not just changes in the land but also the shifts in our culture as the focus of environmental issues and concerns changes over time.

In the different voices of the Ecological Reflections Project, we can listen in on an unfolding conversation of writers engaging with the same place and with one another. As writers from different academic and geographical backgrounds observe, record, and digest what they see in the same place, their reflections inevitably take various forms—from nature journals, to natural history essays and ecological studies, to poems and songs; there is even a work of fiction in David Gessner's story fragment, inspired by the dramatic setting of the Dark Cliffy Spot. This interweaving of various forms suggests something of the wide-ranging nature of the conversations taking place, but the common theme tying the pieces together is the attempt to find meaning and significance—personal, cultural, spiritual, ecological—through encounters with a specific place in a process of sustained close attention. The more we look—and the more angles we look from—the more we can see.

Given the polyphonic nature of the ongoing conversations and the different academic backgrounds of the writers collected here, the Ecological Reflections Project also reflects a key theme of the burgeoning fields of environmental studies and environmental science by highlighting the value of interdisciplinarity. One point demonstrated by the project is that writers and scholars bring not only different individual perspectives but different disciplinary ones as well. A biologist will see something different from a poet or a historian, and a visiting westerner will see something different than a native easterner does. The most complete picture of the landscape is achieved in the juxtaposition of different visions. We know all about the value of diversity in the natural world—diversity of habitats, species, and genetic heritage. This project suggests as well the value of diversity in how we perceive the natural world—diversity in terms of individual perspective, region of origin, and academic background.

Along with its interdisciplinary dimension, the Ecological Reflections Project taps into other current concepts and trends in

literary ecocriticism and the environmental sciences. So-called sec-
ond-wave ecocritics have shifted their scholarly attention from issues
of wilderness preservation to what Scott Hess has called "everyday
nature"—that is, the environments that we encounter in our everyday
lives, and the ways in which our everyday activities affect the natural
world (the food we eat, the waste we create, and so on).[3] The focus,
then, is far more likely to be on urban and suburban environments
than on wilderness, and the point is to move beyond perceptions
of the human and the "natural" as separate categories. This shift of
attention is evident in the work of environmental historians and
nature writers in the past decade or so.

These movements toward reintegration of the human and the natural have special relevance to the Ecological Reflections Project. Each
of the sites serves to illustrate the ways in which human activity has
in some way shaped or changed the landscape—or is now required
to manage and protect it. At the Raptor Center, the creatures that
may seem to us the very emblems of the wild—eagles, hawks, owls,
kestrels—are kept in cages except when they go on tour to local school
groups, their care and feeding costs covered by donors. These are birds
that because of injury would not survive in the wild. Twin Bridges is
the site of a former beaver dam just above the highest reaches of a
lake created by a human dam—and there is that sign giving visitors
a lesson on "reading the forested landscape," dropping hints not only
about the presence of beavers but also about the historical presence
of the tanning industry. At the Sawmill Site, while it may take some
looking as the forest grows taller and wilder by the year, you can find
evidence of the mill that was there a little over a century ago—evidence in the form of a curving ditch from the old mill race and a
jumbled pile of stones where the mill itself stood, at the point where
the race returns to the creek. At the Chestnut Orchard, the "forest"
is behind a fence—not because it is a prisoner but in an attempt to
keep out deer as researchers try to backcross native American chestnut trees with exotic Chinese chestnuts in order to get a tree that
is mostly American chestnut but with the Chinese chestnut's resistance to chestnut blight. The Bluebird Trail goes along and above a
couple of meadows that are mown specifically to help create ideal
bluebird habitat. The Lake Trail is a trail that is obviously laid out
and mapped and kept clear by people, and it circumambulates a lake

that is a creation of the human-made dam. Each of the sites, then, speaks to the ways in which human activity is evident as influence or shaping force—and even to the ways in which human stewardship is necessary in order to retain some semblance of "wildness" in natural environments. Perhaps the one exception to the many ways in which these sites illustrate the mediating effects of human management—all in the name of saving whatever vestiges of wilderness we can—is the Dark Cliffy Spot. (It also happens to be the most remote spot on the ecoreflections tour—and my personal favorite.)

Our hope is that the Ecological Reflections Project at Shaver's Creek—and the initial venture along these lines at Oregon State's Andrews Experimental Forest—might serve as a model for similar experiments in coming to know and appreciate region. Both sites maintain websites containing their writings—the Shaver's Creek reflections are compiled on a webpage called "Creek Journals: A Long-Term Ecological Reflections Project," and the Andrews reflections at "Forest Log." The Andrews site also lists arts- and humanities-oriented ecological reflection projects at other locations.⁴ Several of those are taking place at the designated sites in the NSF Long-Term Ecological Reflections Project, many of them at present seeming to focus on visual art exhibits and a few others highlighting the written word. In Arizona, the project led to a book called *The Sonoran Desert: A Literary Field Guide*. At the Harvard Forest in Massachusetts, the project led to a book of elegiac tribute called *Hemlock: A Forest Giant on the Edge*.⁵ At all of these places, the point is partially to celebrate the virtues of a particular landscape—but even more to promote the hope that people everywhere else will pay more attention to their own local landscapes, in all the places people care deeply about: native prairie in Kansas, tropical forest in Hawaii, the rugged coast of Nova Scotia, the Rockies or the southern Appalachians or the desert Southwest. The purpose of such endeavors in a nutshell: to notice and understand and reinforce our connections to the landscapes we cherish, to trace changes in the land, and to save what we can while we can.

N40 40.010', W077 54.400'. Elevation 844 ft.

That was the reading on my borrowed GPS unit thirteen years ago at my first ecoreflection stop at the Twin Bridges. Here's how to get there: first, make your way to the center of Pennsylvania, toward the last earthen ripple of the Ridge and Valley country. As the geological story goes, a couple of hundred million years ago, continents collided and made these ripples, as if someone had kicked the edge of a continental carpet. That thousand-foot ripple to the northwest—that's Bald Eagle Ridge, and it is the last ridge of the Ridge and Valley Province of the Appalachian Mountains. Across that next valley rises the Allegheny Front and beyond that is the Allegheny Plateau. This is Centre County, and the biggest town here is State College, and you get one guess about what institution has brought most of the population here. It is the home of Penn State University, located in the middle of the state, some say, so as to be equally inaccessible from everywhere else in the state. Shaver's Creek Environmental Center and Stone Valley Recreation Area are about twelve miles south of the University Park campus, over Tussey Ridge (second to last of the Ridge and Valley ridges—at the summit you cross into Huntingdon County), past hunting camps and an old iron furnace. Park your imaginary car at the Environmental Center on Discovery Road, check out the educational exhibits inside, and admire the birds in the Raptor Center cages out back. Then cross the parking lot to descend on the Lake Trail. In just a few minutes, you can take a trail to the right to cross the northern end of Lake Perez on a boardwalk or go left to get to the Twin Bridges site, with the bridges crossing Shaver's Creek, running down from the southeast side of Tussey Ridge.

From here, it'll take four or five hours to hike to all the sites—longer if you go with one of the excellent naturalists from the Environmental Center, who will pause to identify every bird call they hear (and they will hear a lot!). Four of the sites are accessible via side trips from your circumambulation of the lake via the Lake Trail. Our instruction to most of the visiting writers is to try to visit two a day over the course of a workweek, spending several hours at each site listening, looking, thinking, and writing.

In my first official "reflecting" visit thirteen years ago, I spent some time sitting on one of the bridges just listening to the sibilants of the stream's flow and watching a trout do its magic trick of holding steady in the current, facing upstream so it could see what was coming at him—a lesson for us all there, it seemed to me. I thought about the whole metaphor of "reading" the landscape, as if it were text, a topic of special interest to someone like me who teaches literature for a living. As someone who teaches literature classes in an environmental studies curriculum, I often feel compelled to defend the importance of literature. Our students sometimes seem to want to focus on only the science part of their education—they want to learn how to use GIS (geographic information systems) technology, how to do water testing and wetlands delineation, and so on. Those are all valuable things, and students are quick to see the value of that sort of learning—a lot quicker than they are to see the value of environmental history or ethics or literature. In trying to explain to them why literature matters, I often speak about the importance of being culturally literate, of learning to be skilled with language and to become better critical and creative thinkers—the familiar arguments my students have heard before—but more and more over the years I have come to defend literature's importance by invoking evolutionary theory. If the evolutionary mandate of all living things is to survive and reproduce, how in the world did literature become a cross-cultural universal among our species? People everywhere, at all times and in all places, tell stories and play with language. Why would that behavior persist? If it were a useless thing that only distracted from the necessary work of getting food and shelter, why wouldn't those who insisted on wasting their time telling (and listening to) stories have dropped out of the gene pool?

There are lots of answers to the question of how literature and other arts might provide an adaptive advantage—as a means of sexual selection, for example, since the storyteller could show off his mental agility and impress possible mates (which might account for a lot of crappy love songs as well in more contemporary times). But as I sat by Shaver's Creek that long ago afternoon, I thought mostly about the way I had "read" the lesson of the trout holding steady in the current, facing upstream, as if it were some sort of symbol. I was interpreting what I saw, finding meaning in it. That, of course, is what literature always requires of us—to fill in the artfully placed gaps in the text in order to understand it more deeply, to find meaning in experience. Why did the protagonist do that? What is the villain up to now? How will Sherlock Holmes solve the crime? And think of why that skill would have been useful to our Paleolithic ancestors—to understand how others might think, to be really proficient in a nuanced use of language, but most of all to be really skilled at reading signs. How much longer till the berries ripen? Which way did the elk go, and how long since it left that track? What sort of rock is best for knapping into tools? Why did all those birds lift off from those trees over there? Though I knew it was more pun than etymology, it occurred to me on my first reflecting visit that the word *language* sounds like *land gauge*, and that the vital skill that might have made literature so useful to our kind—and still does—is interpretation.

Somewhere along the line, several years after that day I spent listening to the stream and watching the trout, the writers in the Long-Term Ecological Reflections Project began to refer to themselves as "LTERPreters," a coinage that took hold after we started using the acronym LTERP for Long-Term Ecological Reflections Project. That seems so apt. Each of the writers here is an interpreter of the land, using language to gauge the land, to tell us something about what the land holds for us in terms of meaning.

A hundred years ago, most of the forests in Stone Valley had already been sacrificed—gone first to fuel charcoal furnaces for the iron industry, then for timber, then—hemlocks especially—finally taken for their bark for the tanning industry. The Rudy Sawmill was no longer in operation, and neither was the Rudy brothers' still—which remained a source of revenue for the Rudys longer than the sawmill had. There were still forests, perhaps, up on the ridges and to the east around the Seven Mountains area. There, remnant forests a century ago were placed under the protection of the new Pennsylvania Department of Forests and Waters (forerunner of the Pennsylvania state forest system), established in 1895 under the leadership of Joseph Rothrock, namesake of Rothrock State Forest, the state forest responsible for much of the protected forest in the area. In the valley, though, and especially in the area of Shaver's Creek, subsistence farmers tried to make a go of it. It wouldn't be long before many of those farms would fail during the Great Depression, and the federal government would take ownership of the land and lease it to Penn State University for use by the School of Forestry. In the 1930s, workers from a nearby Civilian Conservation Corps camp built the log structure that now serves as the main building and offices for the Shaver's Creek Environmental Center. The CCC workers probably also planted the larch trees just past the parking lot at the start of the

Lake Trail. A hundred years ago, surely nobody would have imagined that one day there would be a lake in the center of the valley (the dam to create Lake Perez was completed in 1960), or that what was once working forest, farm, and field would become an environmental center (which happened in the 1970s).[6]

And what will be here a hundred years from now? Perhaps it is foolish to try to imagine the changes, and surely some of them will entail some loss. But whatever those changes are, they will be documented, recorded, pondered, and responded to, thanks to this project and the people who support it. Maybe a hundred years from now a researcher will turn to these ecological reflections to see what sorts of birds or wildflowers or amphibians populated the area, what the shores of the creek looked like, or how big the trees were. While the changes will be never-ending, and any attempt to record them necessarily incomplete, what we can hope for in the rest of this century is to do our best to learn the forest by seeing it from as many perspectives as possible—and to keep looking. Our own plans are to continue to seek diversity in the writers and scholars we invite to the ecological reflection sites—an ornithologist, an environmental philosopher, an environmental economist, a forester, a climatologist, perhaps—to sit and wonder and think about what they see. It's not exactly the Star Trek mission—"to boldly go where no man has gone before." Rather, it's something more like "follow in the footprints of others, see what else there is to see, record the changes, see what we can, while we can." Why? To better understand and appreciate what is there. What is still there.

It's a beginning.

NOTES

1. See Charles Goodrich, "Entries into the Forest," in *Forest Under Story: Creative Inquiry in an Old-Growth Forest*, edited by Nathaniel Brodie, Charles Goodrich, and Frederick J. Swanson (Seattle: University of Washington Press, 2016), 7, 9, 11, 13.

2. Eric Prieto, "Geocriticism Meets Ecocriticism: Bertrand Westphal and Environmental Thinking," in *Ecocriticism and Geocriticism: Overlapping Territories in Environmental and Spatial Literary Studies*, edited by Robert T. Tally Jr. and Christine M. Battista (New York: Palgrave, 2016), 24–25; Bertrand Westphal, foreword, in *Geocritical Explorations: Space, Place, and Mapping in Literary and Cultural Studies*, edited

by Robert T. Tally Jr. (New York: Palgrave, 2011), xiv.

3. Scott Hess, "Imagining an Everyday Nature," *Interdisciplinary Studies in Literature and Environment* 17, no. 1 (2010): 85–112.

4. See the complete collection of ecological reflections at Shaver's Creek, titled "Creek Journals," at http://www .shaverscreek.org/about-us/initiatives /long-term-ecological-reflections-proj ect/. For the complete collection of the ecological reflections project at the Andrews Forest, titled "Forest Log," see http://www.andrewsforestlog.org /category/writing. See www.ecological reflections.com for news of the other

ecological reflection projects in addition to the Shaver's Creek project.

5. For information on these and other results from ecological reflections projects, see Charles Goodrich and Frederick J. Swanson, "Long-Term Ecological Reflections: Art Among Science Among Place," *Terrain. org: A Journal of the Built + Natural Environments,* August 28, 2016, http:// www.terrain.org/2016/guest-editorial /long-term-ecological-reflections/.

6. Information on the history of Shaver's Creek and Stone Valley comes from Jacy Marshall-McKelvey's *The History of Shaver's Creek,* forthcoming on the Shaver's Creek website.

Twin Bridges

TRAILHEAD NOTE

Let us go then, you and I, Dear Reader, and afoot and lighthearted take to the open road—which in our case will take the form of a series of dirt paths that will lead us through the Stone Valley forests to the eight ecoreflection sites. It'll take us a good part of the day, covering about seven or eight miles, up ridges and down, to the lake and around, across streams and meadows. We'll want to pause regularly to contemplate the past and savor the present moment, identify trees and bird calls, admire occasional views of Lake Perez or distant ridges, listen to rustlings in the brush and the patter of our own footfalls, share stories as we go.

Our first stop is the Twin Bridges, and to get there you pick up the Lake Trail right at the Environmental Center, first heading past a stand of European larches. These were probably planted by the Civilian Conservation Corps in the 1930s, perhaps the same CCC unit that built the oldest log section of the Environmental Center itself. Passing those larches, I can't help but think of them as the "and now for something completely different" trees, from the old Monty Python routine. The larch is indeed something completely different, an evergreen that is not in fact ever green, a conifer that drops its needles in the winter. Within a few hundred feet, a trail to the right leads to the boardwalk over the farthest reach of Lake Perez (farthest from the dam, that is), but staying on the Lake Trail we wind through deciduous forest, including a large white oak with a bench conveniently placed under it. In less than ten minutes we reach a hemlock grove where a sign cites Tom Wessels's classic *Reading the Forested Landscape* in giving a few clues about the environmental history of the spot where we are standing. The sign talks about how "pillows" and "cradles" are formed by wind-toppled trees, and points out how a line of hemlock roots speaks to the belowground presence of a "nurse" log, perhaps a hemlock that was cut and stripped of its bark, which was used for leather tanning when this area was home to the Erb family more than a hundred years ago. The fallen hemlock that became a nurse log clearly never made it to the Rudy Sawmill, which lay a quarter mile or so upstream.

Conical notches in other hemlock trunks, both standing and fallen, give the most obvious clue as to the area's more recent environmental history—beavers were at work here, girdling the hemlocks to make room for more preferred species. The beavers' presence also accounts for the clearing around the bifurcated creek just beyond the hemlocks. The clearing indicates that a beaver dam must have been just downstream of this spot, and this area had been part of their pond. As it happens, just a few hundred feet downstream of this spot is also where the stream enters Lake Perez, the result of another dam installed by a different busy species.

The two branches of Shaver's Creek that slice through that open area beyond the hemlocks is spanned by two plank bridges that were washed out by high water and replaced within the first ten years of the Ecological Reflections Project. In short, this little area has undergone an awful lot of change over the course of the last five or six generations. At the same time, there is persistence: though the still-standing hemlocks surrounding the Wessels sign are not big around in the trunk—maybe half a foot in diameter—a core sample has revealed that they too have been here for more than a century. That blend of persistence and change seems to constitute the common theme of the ecological reflections emanating from this spot. This is a spot that makes us recognize that human dam builders are not alone in their impulse to effect dramatic changes in the land. But this too is a spot that encourages the writers who have visited to take a longer view of the passage of time, and to marvel at the way forests persist amid the constant change. Some trees fall or are cut down in their prime, but others live long and not only prosper but regenerate; people come and go, bridges and dams may come and go, but the stream runs on.

On Orange Teeth and Busy Beavers

SCOTT WEIDENSAUL (2006)

The interpretive sign, dusted with yellow hemlock needles, says, "Reading the Shaver's Creek Landscape," and it talks of pillows and cradles, of nurse logs and windthrow. But when I look around and read the history of this spot, I see a landscape sculpted not by storms but by four sharp, bright orange incisors.

It is an early evening in late August, a time of the day (and a time of the year) that is a winding down, an ending of things. The light streams in from the west, low across Lake Perez, and the wind that blew through the day has all but died. Only the leaves in the highest branches of the tulip trees still waggle in the slim breeze; the maples hang motionless, unimpressed, and down near the ground the air is heavy and still.

Like the solstice at some Bronze Age stone circle, the sun cuts a perfect line up the middle of the small creek, illuminating the narrow avenue of meadow that lies among the hemlocks. From where I sit, the jungly growth is backlit, dragonflies with wings like shards of ice coursing among the drooping seed heads of bulrush, and the purple masses of joe-pye with their stalks of whorled leaves, the white gauze of boneset, splashes of crimson cardinal flower, lacy goldenrods, the fuzzy leaves of deer-tongue grass, cobalt lobelias and cattails.

Through the center of this vest-pocket meadow rises a line of dead hemlocks. From the sagging, skeletal branch of one, a flycatcher launches itself to snag a bug, both bird and prey leaving an afterimage of blurred sunlight on my retina as they intersect and merge. The bird perches, green-gray, anonymous. An alder flycatcher, or its look-alike cousin, the willow? No way to say which species, since the bird isn't singing, no *fitz-bew* or *ree-be-o* to declare its allegiance to one branch of the family tree or the other.

Those dead hemlocks are the key to unlocking the recent history of this place. Hemlocks love little streams like this one, the cool, acidic soil that they further steep with their tannic needles, while darkening its banks with diffuse, deep sea-green shadows through which only a few confused sunbeams penetrate.

But dam a stream, as the beavers once did—bring that water up just a few feet, saturate that soil, and the hemlocks die. A hemlock is wasted on a beaver, which turns up its flat nose at the bitter bark, but that won't stop them from killing the hemlocks, flooding them or girdling them to open up the canopy for alders and other more toothsome growth. So the hemlocks drowned, grew leafless and largely branchless, casting their reflections in the dark, still water of the beaver pond. The stream slowed, pooled, its current lost to hunger, to chewing, to an obsessive rodent obstructionism that finds the sound of flowing water anathema that must be plugged and silenced. The hemlocks died, but the bluegills were happy.

And presumably so were the beavers, for a time. But food never lasts forever, and neither do beaver dams. The colony ate itself out of hearth and home, as they always do, and left or died. No beaver came snuffling after the leaks to plug them, no one stopped up the hateful trickles; the dam grew more porous, until the spring rains took it out. By then, though, the orange teeth that first cut the wood and girdled the hemlocks were scattered in the muddy bottom of Lake Perez, fallen from the sightless skulls of long-dead beavers. The stream cut down through the muck that had accumulated over the years and found its channel again, and the thick bed of silt that remains blooms with an exuberance that makes me think it's making up for lost time—and maybe in foreknowledge of how limited its own run will be.

Of course, the real busy beavers in this valley were Lawrence Perez and his colleagues, back in 1960, moving tons of earth to plug Shaver's Creek with a dam a little more permanent than the maple logs and alder branches of the beavers. But only a little more permanent. One day, maybe far off by the measure of humans, that plug will be pulled, too; the stream will find its old channel, not just for a year or two, while engineers tinker with the dam, but for good. The rich silt will bloom, and the plants will give thanks for the steel teeth that made their meadow. The forest will bide its time, as forests can afford to do, knowing that like beaver dams—like human dams—meadows are not forever, either.

Dams and Lushness

DAVID GESSNER (2012)

June 10

Dams are very much on my mind. I wonder if most easterners are aware of how central dams are to almost every enviro fight in the West. Yesterday afternoon, I spoke to my old Colorado roommate, Rob Bleibery, who now lives in Grand Junction and fights to put land into trust. He told me that in the center of town there is a memorial for Wayne Aspinall, the congressman who served as a lifelong roadblock to environmental legislation, or rather as a guardian who would let some enviro legislation pass, but only if a new dam was attached. The memorial shows a picture of some fields being irrigated and features this line: "In the West when you touch water you touch everything."

Of course, this is not the West. That was wonderfully apparent on our first day of hiking. Just two days before, I'd been hiking down dusty moonscape trails, no water in sight, dryness the dominant theme. How strange to encounter the lushness of the Bluebird Trail. I am reading about the old-time explorers of Yellowstone, and there are many things they have seen that I never will. But they will never have the uniquely modern experience that I just had: walking one day in the dry West and the next in the wet East.

I have been having a correspondence with Wendell Berry (trying to find a time to visit him), and I sent him a book proposal. I wrote in the proposal that the West does not recover as well as "the green East." He took issue with this, rightly, pointing to the scars left by mining. But, comparatively, I stand by my point. In the West we see life spilling into every niche when we look up at a cactus growing—alone!—a thousand feet up a canyon wall. But the same point is made here by sheer profusion. Trails spill over with green, meadows are reclaimed, foundations overrun with grass and leaf. Green in the West is a precarious color, with only a tentative hold on the sore landscape. This is true even along waterfalls, where after the thin line of huddling cottonwoods, the land returns to dust. Here instead we have mud. "I prefer the mush woods to the arid desert," said W. J. Bate. Well, he'd like it here. Lush.

So, dams and lushness. At Twin Bridges, Ian pointed out how the dead hemlocks had given birth to new trees. At the Grand Canyon, I could point up and say, "That rock was there fifty thousand years ago." But here everything is constantly growing over, and out of, everything else. Succession is happening in front of our eyes. The layering of this place fascinates. Trees grow out of trees and past out of present. We saw this both in the gone beaver dam and at the mill site. Both hold hints of what they were, but only hints. If Mr. Rudy or the beaver came back, they would long for the good old days. Both saw this creek not as a place for hiking and taking nature notes but as source for livelihood, a flowing artery out of which they made what they were.

It just so happens that one of the few books I brought with me this week was *The Complete Poems of Robert Frost*. I hadn't thought much about Frost in a while, but I threw it in my bag. One of the only poems I ever memorized is "Directive," which speaks to the mill and the dam:

> Back out of all this now too much for us,
> Back in a time made simple by the loss
> Of detail, burned, dissolved, and broken off
> Like graveyard marble sculpture in the weather.[1]

Frost was a depressive, and if you think about this "dissolving" too much, you might be inclined to follow him down this road. In the West, an Anasazi makes a mark on a stone and we see a galloping pronghorn ten thousand years later. Here, an old mill is swallowed up by trees and grass and all we can make out is an echoing shape, an imagined sluice. It is the key to this land. The old is covered and forgotten. Or remembered, but only faintly. We dig into old records. We re-create. We never see it preserved as what it was. "Directive" again:

> There is a house that is no more a house
> Upon a farm that is no more a farm . . .

And a mill that is no more a mill. As for many of the trees here, we can ask with Frost: "Where were they all not twenty years ago?"

Maybe, in this case, twenty is closer to a hundred, but the point is the same. The time before has been swallowed up, lost, the new time growing out of it until it too will be lost. In a sense, the whole thing is one giant nurse log.

But I've wandered far from dams.

I don't know the history of these beavers, why they, or their progeny, moved on to greener pastures. Perhaps the human beavers, Mr. Perez most prominently, backed up their waters with their own dam. What does a beaver do then? Flop over land in search of a new creek?

While I don't know these beavers specifically, I have thought some about the species. I suppose it is generally acknowledged that they win the silver medal when it comes to building things that affect and alter landscapes, most particularly riverine landscapes. Standing atop the Glen Canyon Dam the other day—at 710 feet high it is the second-tallest in the United States—I felt a sort of awe, not just for the dizzying height, but for the fact that within the order of *Homo sapiens* there was a subset who could build something like that. They are certainly not members of my tribe. As I have mentioned elsewhere, the best my artsy tribe could do would be to throw a few logs across a creek. It seems to me that they have more in common with beavers than with me.

The beaver is not just the embodiment of the builder and engineer, however. It is also a handy human symbol for the workaholic. Busy as . . . I've mentioned elsewhere that Wallace Stegner was fond of the metaphor, applied to habitual human workers, of beavers needing to keep chewing/working lest they impale themselves on their own teeth. "It's easy to be lazy," said Stegner. "But I don't seem to be able to do it." He particularly liked to apply the beaver metaphor to writers, and when you see this dam that is no longer a dam, the metaphor turns potentially gloomy: you work and you work and no one remembers. (Or maybe someone remembers, but he's just a nature writer paid to come here and take nature notes.)

Beaver's humanness and human's beaverness are nicely illustrated by having the mill and dam so close. Obviously, they might be close in proximity but not temporally. Mr. Rudy would have little tolerance for a bunch of water rats clogging up his stream. And Mr. Beaver would not have enjoyed the no doubt befouled water flowing out of the sluiceway of Mr. Rudy.

But one more word about human's beaverness, since these are supposed to be ecological reflections, and this quality is an important one to understand in the context of today's ecological fight. We can rail against our tendency to build, to progress, and say, "You should not be that way!" But maybe it is better to accept our beaverliness, and work from there.

Let me explain . . .

One of Thoreau's great lessons was to leave well enough alone. Which may be the single hardest thing for human beings to do. We are tinkerers, curious monkeys, busy beavers. When something is good, we want to make it better. But it is through the tinkering that we end up damming our sacred places.

So. What is to be done? How do we quiet ourselves and put our tools briefly aside? How do we overcome minds programmed to look for better ways, better places? Is that the next step in evolution?

It doesn't seem to be. Even naturalists, like the interns I walked with on Friday, are natural acquirers. They are hunters for facts, for knowledge. Which maybe holds a secret. Maybe we cannot stop our never-sleeping hungry minds. But maybe we can choose our tools better. Maybe we can focus all that energy in a direction that does good, not harm. When I see five kids, ambitious and hungry in their own way, focusing that hunger on becoming better naturalists, I think it is deeply encouraging. It is not my own relationship with nature (as these notes attest) but one that I have come to admire more and more, as I spend time with naturalists. It pays to remember that Thoreau too was a natural tinkerer, inventor, builder. (In fact, he might be the most famous homebuilder in history.) Given that his inner beaver was so strong, it is all but miraculous that he is known best for retiring. For not doing.

There is hope here. To be ambitious, yes, but to strive to be better, not more. To sharpen and whittle and clarify our aims.

My own goal is to become less ambitious. (But even here, in this cabin in the woods, the words spill out.)

NOTE

1. Robert Frost, "Directive," in *The Poetry of Robert Frost: The Collected Poems, Complete and Unabridged*, edited by Edward Connery Lathem (New York: Henry Holt, 1969), 377–78.

The Insistence of Forests

HANNAH INGLESBY (2014)

The coolness of the night pools, leftover, in all the places sun doesn't touch. The sounds are those of ripened summer: the aeronautics of flies, an insect call like an ostinato of tiny bells, and the intermittent swell of cicadas that crests and recedes. Almost noon, the light through the hemlocks lounges on hillocks of moss, in splashed languor. It's a grove that is secret-feeling, as if worlds could open up if you entered between the right two trees.

In the late August cant of the air and the light, there's a sense of time's fullness. Sitting here on the soft earth, my back against a trunk, I feel accompanied by the past. Children's voices replay silently in my recent memory, called up by the miniature huts of sticks and moss still standing here and there among the trees. Only a few weeks ago, I led groups of gap-toothed kids, who were happy most moments to be in the woods at summer camp. They might now be buying new clothes and sharpening pencils for school, or gearing up for Grange Fair, but a part of them remains behind in the gestures of their play. The forest harbors these leavings graciously, reclaiming the little houses to the earth as the weather and the decomposers do their work of disassembling.

Memories stack like strata. Now I'm recalling one camp morning running with a fellow counselor, Vireo, to Twin Bridges. She'd been grasping at our morning meeting for material to use that day for a bird-tracks activity. Then my thoughts flashed to the clay on the banks of Shaver's Creek. We carved the clay with ice-cream scoops into plastic bowls, which we toted back up to the Environmental Center. Later that day, after the kids had pressed tracks into trays of clay, Vireo walked with her campers back to Twin Bridges, where they ceremoniously returned the gray earth.

A catbird is mewing. Its rusty insistence punctuates the sound of the creek. If not for time and rot, how many feet of hemlock needles would be piled here, from how many years of growth and casting off? One of my campers lost a tooth while on the trail and we tucked it into her sandwich box. The tall joe-pye weeds hint at how far we've come this summer, though more growth will arrive before the slope is covered with snow. Past high waters have left swaths of sticks by the creek. A log is beaver-chewed. Lichens color trees as if they are canvases in slow motion, the invisible painter working by increments. If I knew how to look, I could tell you what walked where. To the attuned noses of animals, this scene is a map of scents.

We need forests in many ways; among them is the sense they give us of our place in time. Forests hold the depth of seasons upon seasons, what with all the stages of striving and senescence commingling. The leavings of yesterday waltz with the births of today. The tree I lean on has been leaned on before. Patience presides. Old cathedrals come close to attaining this quality of memory in balance, prayers imbuing the air with holiness and the tall columns causing us to crane our necks. But unlike the manmade, the forest regenerates. It insists up through the cracks where we hold it back. What falls down grows up. Our spirits need that doggedness.

In Search of Signs

MICHAEL P. BRANCH (2014)

This is the first site I've visited, and as a neophyte here I am look-ing for a way to access and communicate with it, just as I do when meeting a person for the first time. I take a quick reconnaissance, scanning the treetops, the dense vegetation, noting the newish look of the double bridge, the water as it slides along the verdant banks of the nearby stream. Give me a sign! And, like all people looking for a sign, I get mine. Only this sign has been offered not by God but by man. That man turns out to be Josh, a gifted naturalist who has been coming to Shaver's Creek since he was a kid and has now come full circle to join the staff. Josh made this sign many years ago while working as an intern here, and the plastic laminate installed to protect the panel is pretty well splintered away by now, exposing the wooden frame. Nature has begun to break down this cultural artifact, just as it does the fallen trees that the sign exists to explain. Josh's sign, which is all about change over time in the forest, is itself becoming an illustration of such change.

A sign can't help itself. It structures your experience of a place. It says, "Stand here." "Ask these questions." "See the place in this way." "Remember this idea." "Question how this fits into the bigger pic-ture." It also—and here is the most important part—*puts text into the woods*. That is, a sign forces you to become a *reader*. But to be a reader also means to pay attention, at least momentarily, to something other than the land itself. Perhaps while reading this sign I have missed my only opportunity to have a second glance at what might have been a pileated woodpecker arcing through the canopy. But the compensa-tion is that every line I read on Josh's sign helps me to see more when I look up from it. This, I think, is what all good books are intended to do. We read them and then return to the world with the hope that we can see more than we could before. If we lose a moment or two with our heads down, we are rewarded by the new eyes we bring when we lift our faces to the world again.

Josh's sign is a single-panel book, and a very good one. It explains with admirable clarity a few core principles that can help us to "better understand the history and future of our local landscape," which is precisely what I've come here to do. It offers a few terms, but does so in ways that are compelling, imaginative, and accessible. In reading this sign I am struck by how our understanding of the more-than-human world shows everywhere the signs of our own experience. The mounds and divots left by fallen trees are, we learn, referred to as "pillows" and "cradles," respectively. The log that results, if it decomposes at just the right rate—neither too fast nor too slow—will nurture a new generation of seedlings and is thus referred to as a "nurse" log. *Pillow, cradle, nurse.* These are words we not only understand but also feel. They resonate because they have imaginative power that we recognize from our own domestic lives. My daughters back home in the high desert are seven and eleven years old, and yet I now find my mind wandering back to their birth and infancy. They too were nursed and cradled, and I have a clear memory of placing them carefully between pillows to protect them from rolling off the bed.

This place, as Josh's sign attests, can help us think about the agents and evidence of change. It seems to me that the places where we live our lives, like the lives themselves, are constantly racing into the future. If the decomposition of a nurse log doesn't appear to be a process that is racing, perhaps that is only because we have not adjusted our scale of perception to appreciate the change that is constantly taking place here. The sign also notes that in the 1870s Emanuel and Rebecca Erb lived here with their eight children. That family changed this place, and it must also have changed them. I find it difficult to imagine what their experience was like, living in the wake of the Civil War, along the banks of this lovely creek. They are all long gone from this earth now, but the signs of their passing through are still marked on the land.

What is it that is so compelling about the two bridges at this site? There are bridges over just about every creek, rivulet, and muddy spot along the trail, but there is something about these two bridges— something, I think, about the way they are somehow both together and apart. Are they the two halves of a single bridge, since they cross the same creek, or are they two bridges? The LTERP, devised by my friend Ian Marshall in collaboration with the Shaver's Creek folks, calls them Twin Bridges—not Twin Bridge or the Twin Bridges, but just Twin Bridges, as if to acknowledge the duality of this singular place. I suspect that the pleasure may be in looking up while crossing a bridge only to see another bridge ahead that needs to be crossed. What is the natural thing to do when crossing a bridge? Stop in the middle to have a look down and around. But when I pause on either bridge, I see the bridge ahead and have the immediate urge to cross it. I know the Wordsworthian thing to do would be to stand or sit at the center of one of these bridges and contemplate the stream. Instead, I find myself crossing the forked creek across both bridges, then turning on my heel to do it again in the other direction.

And it is worse than that. Not only am I crossing and recrossing these two bridges like a madman, but because I love the way they sway a little I am also rocking the bridges to produce a pleasing sensation of lateral movement. If anyone up in the hills is observing my weird dance through their birding binoculars, they may feel compelled to let the Shaver's Creek staff know that a strange man is losing his mind down by the creek. What in hell is wrong with this guy? Keep the school groups away! Cross, sway. Cross, sway. Recross, sway. Recross, sway. Re-recross, sway. Re-recross, sway. I'm aware, of course, that some poor day hiker may come upon me doing this and feel uncomfortable, but I'm prepared to explain myself if necessary. First, I'll say, "It's okay. I'm not a troll. I'm just a writer." Most reasonable people are willing to accept an urge toward creativity as an adequate excuse for eccentric behavior. That failing, I intend to stand in the middle of the bridge, face the hiker squarely, and explain, "I am from the Great Basin Desert and have never seen water before. I am here to contemplate change and time in this place. I am turning these bridges into metaphors of the past and future. One is the bridge of life and the other the bridge of death. I am the ghost of Emanuel Erb!" Or, perhaps, just this: "I have come to give you one small gift: the story of the time you encountered a ranting writer at Twin Bridges." Once a place is wedded with story, it becomes unforgettable.

Josh's sign, the swaying of the bridges, the LTERP itself—each asks us to think about what this place will be like in a future that is sufficiently distant in time that I will by then be hoisting pints with Emanuel Erb. I'll hazard a guess, though. These blackberries will still be here, blossoming in their brambles, and so will this twining Virginia creeper, and the slender grasses that rise near the gravel bar at the stream's edge. But this bridge that is two bridges will be gone, carried away by flood or by the flood of years. Josh's sign will be gone. But there will be other signs here, forever and always. If we're lucky, there will be still be folks around here who can read them—or, at least, somebody who has an earnest wish to learn.

The Sawmill Site

TRAILHEAD NOTE

Crossing the Twin Bridges, the intrepid circumambulator of the eco-logical reflections sites comes to a trailhead T just on the other side of Shaver's Creek. Eventually, your path will go right, toward Lake Perez, but first take a detour to the left, upstream. The path—now the Sawmill Trail—winds away from and then along and above the creek for about half a mile. A small, slick-when-wet wooden bridge crosses an intermittent tributary, and on the left is the site of the old Rudy family sawmill. Of course you wouldn't know what you were looking at if you didn't have the explanatory sign nearby—or a guide to point out the shallow ditch of what was once a millrace, and the jumble of rocks down the slope where the ditch meets the creek. Those blocks of stone must have been part of the building foundation for the waterwheel that powered the mill. Just downstream of the mill site is a deep, trouty-looking pool in a curve of the creek.

It's an attractive spot, but it's not so much what you can see now that has caught the imagination of the ecoreflectors who have vis-ited here. Rather, it's the haunt of history, the fact that people much like us once busied themselves making a living out of this patch of forest—and the sense of surprise, too, at how relatively quickly the human presence is being erased by the forest, doing what forests do. What fascinates about the reflections at the Sawmill Site is the way the writers circle around the same historical facts about the Rudy family and—inspired perhaps by the imagined image of a waterwheel that made its last groaning turn a century and a half ago—see not the past disappeared but evidence of cycles of depletion, loss, and return.

The Mill and the Hemlocks

SCOTT WEIDENSAUL (2006)

Shaver's Creek is a ghost of its spring self, its bones laid bare, only capillaries of water flowing between the dry stones of its bed. Its desiccated voice is hushed by drought. But the millrace that runs in from the east—the straight, shallow swale through forest—lies entirely mute, robbed of its water by time.

The old Rudy family sawmill sat on a dry bench about fifteen feet above the creek, sited with an eye to the worst of times, high enough to avoid all but the heaviest floods. But it wasn't high water that did it in. Except for some scattered wall stones, nothing remains except the channel of the millrace, softened by history and shadowed by a forest of young hemlocks and older hardwoods, the ground sparsely covered in Christmas ferns, ground cedar, the glossy ovates of Canada mayflower leaves, and a few tall jack-in-the-pulpits.

I find the hemlocks an ironic touch.

This would have been a forest of tremendous hemlocks, 250 years ago. Something like the Alan Seeger Natural Area is today, across the way a few miles—one of those teasing scraps of old growth for which we're grateful nowadays, big trees but not gigantic ones (monstrous trees were a feature of western forests, not the East), an understory of rhododendron, with light gaps where some decrepit ancient had cracked in a storm and smashed to the ground.

Somewhere nearby, a footpath that rose out of the Standing Stone Creek Valley passed north over the ridge and into the Shaver's Creek Valley, where it would have threaded its way beneath those big hemlocks and white pines, the ground perpetually damp, perpetually shaded.

How long the path existed is anyone's guess—and mine would be: a damned long time. There a hint of that path shown on Nicholas Scull's 1759 map of the Pennsylvania frontier; on his grandson William's map, a much more detailed version drawn in 1770, there is no doubt about the route. It runs from Huntingdon past Tussey Mountain, ending at "Bald Eagle's Nest," the white man's name for

Wapalanewachschiechey, the village of Woapalanne, the Munsee chief known as Bald Eagle.

But I doubt the Munsee first blazed this particular path; the lay of the land, and therefore the best route from point A to point B, doesn't change when one culture supplants another, and I imagine that Paleo-Indians hunting Columbian mammoths and American mastodons through the grassy tundra of Ice Age Pennsylvania would have followed much the same course when they came up this way ten thousand years ago. Likewise the first white settlers, and then the wagon-road builders, and still later the first highway crews pouring macadam, because they all knew a good thing when they trod it.

One of those taking the Standing Stone path north, perhaps with a creased copy of Scull's map carefully tucked inside his linsey-woolsey shirt, was George Rudy, a York County Revolutionary War veteran, accompanied by eleven children, his fecund (and, one would imagine, tired) wife, and his brother Barney.

The Rudys made a place for themselves in Woapalanne's old domain, and may have felt a little smug about that fact; old Bald Eagle had sided with the British, after all, raiding frontier homesteads during the war, before he died at the hands of the brother of a young man Woapalanne himself had scalped.

The Rudys began populating the land with descendants, opening up the forest—grubbing up the saplings, girdling off the big trees, and planting between their dead trunks. At some point, the settlements grew prosperous enough for farmers to want not just a mud-chinked cabin but a house of milled lumber. And the Rudys were ready to oblige; by the 1870s, the Barree Township map shows a mill on Shaver's Creek, and tax records indicate that it was owned by George's grandson, Martin Rudy.

This would not have been a quiet, green-lit forest then, but an open, noisy, dusty place around the mill shed, the air acrid with the smell of sap and sawdust, and the sour, back-of-the-throat bite of fresh-peeled logs; loud with the clank of machinery, the rattle of chains, the whinny of draft horses, the bellowing of oxen. Across the creek stood the Erb homestead—more sunlit fields, the smell of milk cows, wood smoke hanging in the air.

And the rush of water out of the milldam when the sluice gate was opened, the wet slapping of the flutter wheel starting to turn, the saw blade beginning its up-and-down journey, twice each second, biting into the logs that the sawyers fed it. It was hard, sweaty work, wrestling green logs into the teeth of the blade, and it could be dangerous; one New Englander observed that a vertical saw could "pound the unwary into the floor like a shingle nail." But it must have seemed a miracle of gentle technology to the old-timers who knew the tyranny of working a whipsaw by hand. Bad enough to be the top sawyer, standing on a squared-off beam guiding the long, flexible blade along a chalked line, the sun beating on your neck, the muscles in your arms screaming, but worse by far to be the pitman, stuck down below the log in an airless hole, your nose and lungs full of sawdust. And speed! Why, when the sluice ran full and the wheel was spinning, a team could cut forty or fifty boards in a day, six or seven times the lumber that even the best whipsaw artists could produce.

We don't know when the Rudys' mill was first built, though it shows up on local tax rolls in 1861 and disappears from the accounts about twenty years later. Why it closed, I think, is no mystery: the logs ran out. The forest that seemed endless when George and his brood arrived retracted quickly, and by the 1880s the old trees must have been a long wagon drive away from the little mill. The big trees were being cut to the north and west, up along the upper Susquehanna, in huge, highly mechanized operations—teams of professional "wood hicks" to fell them, railroads to haul them, steam mills to cut them on their wickedly efficient band saws, in quantities that beggared the imagination. It may finally have been easier and cheaper to buy lumber from away than to mill it along Shaver's Creek.

The milldam filled in and the mill shed fell to ruin; the piles of sawdust incubated rat snake eggs in the sun until the fast-growing saplings shaded it out, and rot returned it all to the soil. The Erb family place fell to ruin, and the hardwoods of the resurgent forest filled in the once open land. A two-foot-wide tulip tree stands now in the middle of the dry millrace, and the hemlocks crowd in around it. Already, one sees the remains of birches that lost the fight for sunlight with the hemlocks. One day (at least in the normal order of things), the conifers should overtop the hardwoods and reclaim a place that already looks like a spot that Woapalanne would recognize more easily than Martin Rudy.

The last trees to fall in northern and central Pennsylvania were the hemlocks—after the white pines, which had more valuable lumber, after the big oaks and chestnuts, which were sparse on the high ridges and the Allegheny Plateau. The wood was of middling quality; brittle, hard to work, prone to rot and coarsely grained, and the most valuable part of a hemlock was on the outside. A lot of the huge trees, the five-hundred-year-old behemoths, were felled mostly for their bark, stripped off and leached in long, brick-lined pits with hides, the great tannery operations whose stench would blanket a county.

Hemlocks fueled the last great lumber orgy in the state; in just one year, 1896, 1.3 million board feet of virgin hemlock were cut. By the time it was declared the state tree in 1931, there was almost none of the old growth left.

The hemlocks along Shaver's Creek have quite a ways to go to reach those proportions, and they may not make it. They were victorious over the crosscut saw and the mill, over the homesteader and the plow; they have restored the cool bluish shadows, the spring flush of fresh green growth like fireworks on the ends of the branches, and the gentle fall of yellow needles in autumn. But it remains to be seen whether they will withstand the insidious drain of a new pest from Asia. In my part of Pennsylvania, three hours to the southeast, the hemlock woods are a gray and lifeless shadow of themselves. The bug is here, too, in Stone Valley, if for the moment still below the radar, like a virus in the last hours of incubation, before the fever rises.

Extract a core sample from a mucky bog in the Northeast and examine the nearly indestructible fossil pollen grains entombed within, and you'll see that in the postglacial landscape, hemlock was clearly among the most common trees—until forty-eight hundred years ago, when its pollen vanishes. Completely. Hemlocks must have all but disappeared across their range. No one knows why, but presumably a pest (some suspect a looper moth) got here from Asia. Sounds familiar.

After a thousand years, hemlock pollen reappears in the strata of northeastern bogs, and the species—having made its peace with whatever force brought it low—soon reasserted its dominance in eastern forests. The hemlocks clawed their way back then, and they may weather this storm as they did the saw and axe. But a thousand years is a long time to go without the shade of a hemlock forest, and I don't think I can wait that long.

Looking into the Past
The Rudy Sawmill

JACY MARSHALL-MCKELVEY (2012)

Upstream from the marshes on the edge of Lake Perez, Shaver's Creek is a small stream running through dense, shady forest. Its banks often rise a few feet above the water, but in one place, a ditch cuts into the left bank and runs a short distance back into the woods, where a small tributary, often empty of water in dry weather, meets it. A pile of rocks where the ditch meets the stream may be the ruins of a building, but this would not be obvious without knowing that there was once one here. This small trench is rather inconspicuous at first glance, but it is an important relic of local history. At the time of the Civil War, this was the site of a sawmill, owned by four brothers from the Rudy family who shared a tract of land they had inherited.

By the time the Rudy Sawmill opened in approximately 1861, there was already a long history of logging in Huntingdon County. Farmers cut many trees to clear land and for firewood. Near Shaver's Creek, charcoal production for the Monroe and Greenwood iron furnaces probably had a larger impact than sawmills. Still, while not on the vast scale of the logging operations around the West Branch of the Susquehanna, commercial logging was widespread, with dozens of sawmills in the county. The number of mills apparently declined dramatically in the next decade; the Rudy Sawmill would have been one of the later holdouts, perhaps because deforestation occurred more slowly in the remote northern end of the county.

Throughout the time that the sawmill was operating, the Rudy brothers were also farmers. Given this lack of specialization, the logging activities associated with the mill were probably on a small scale. Some sawmills, such as one a few miles away that was owned by the Oaks family in the 1850s and 1860s, were powered by steam at this time, but the ditch beside the stream—the remnant of a millrace, a channel used to divert water toward the mill—suggests that the Rudy Sawmill used the older technology of a waterwheel. This would have powered a mechanical saw that cut the logs into smaller pieces. There currently appears to be a very small, seasonal stream connected to the millrace; this might have supplied water for the mill, but unless it flowed more reliably in the 1800s it might have been difficult to use very often. Alternatively, water from the main creek could have been diverted for a more reliable power source. The millrace is well above the current level of the stream, but a small dam could have raised the water enough to get it to the waterwheel. It is difficult to determine from the remaining records where the logs used came from, or where the lumber was sold. As the owners of a small-scale mill in an area outside the main centers of the timber industry, the Rudys may have sold mainly to local residents, possibly for the construction of farm buildings or furniture.

Major logging operations had originally sent logs to distant markets by floating them down rivers during spring floods; rafts had been used at first, but by the second half of the nineteenth century log drives on the West Branch of the Susquehanna sent enormous numbers of trees downstream with little control, eventually diverting them into storage areas with large booms built in midriver. Railroads were playing an increasingly important role, allowing logging to spread farther from major rivers. But Shaver's Creek was much too small for anything like the log drives on the West Branch of the Susquehanna, and there were no railroads for several miles around; without these transportation options, it seems that the Rudys would have had a limited ability to sell logs far from home on a large scale. Logs might have come to the mill from woodlots on nearby properties, or from the more extensive forests on the slopes of Tussey Mountain. Even to transport them to the mill would have been a challenge; loggers often used teams of oxen to drag fallen trees overland. Wherever they came from, the logs sent to the Rudy Sawmill were probably a relatively small factor in the ongoing deforestation of the area when compared with the charcoal production that fueled the iron furnaces. Many iron furnaces logged the land for miles around several times in a matter of decades.

By the 1870 census, the number of sawmills in Huntingdon County had declined dramatically, probably because of deforestation. Monroe Furnace shut down around the same time; the destruction of the surrounding forests was often a major reason for the abandonment of iron furnaces in Pennsylvania, although in this case the difficulty of transporting metal to distant markets may also have been a factor. However, the Rudy Sawmill managed to hold on for the moment. Furthermore, one of the Rudy brothers' neighbors was probably also cutting trees for profit. Emanuel Erb, who lived just west of the Rudys near the modern Twin Bridges, was listed as a tanner on the 1870 census. Tanners made leather products, but the traditional manufacturing process involved chemicals extracted from the bark of hemlock trees. Tanning practices reflected the wastefulness of nineteenth-century logging; because other trees such as white pine were preferred to hemlock wood, logs cut by tanning operations were often not sold after the bark was removed. Joshua Potter, Shaver's Creek's marketing information coordinator, studied hemlocks near Twin Bridges as a college student and suggested that groups of trees currently growing in straight rows there may have originally taken root on logs left behind by the tanning operation. According to county tax records, Erb lived in the area for only a few years in the late 1860s and early 1870s; by 1880, he seems to have moved to McKean County in northwestern Pennsylvania, where he worked as a carpenter.

While it outlasted many of Huntingdon County's sawmills, the Rudy mill probably shut down around 1882 or 1883, when references to it disappear from tax records. Damage to the local forests could certainly have contributed to its disappearance. Competition from newer technology could also have made the mill less profitable, and the aging Rudy brothers may have simply retired (they continued to operate a distillery, but only for a few years after the sawmill closed). Other logging operations continued nearby; Greenwood Furnace stayed in business until after 1900 making charcoal, and logging companies used small railroads built over rugged terrain to cut trees in the nearby Seven Mountains around the turn of the century. Severe deforestation in much of Pennsylvania eventually inspired government officials to take action; nature reserves, including Rothrock State Forest, were established to ensure the survival of some forested areas. Penn State also conducted logging in the Stone Valley Experimental Forest in the twentieth century, although these operations were planned so as not to wipe out trees over vast areas as earlier generations of loggers had. Still, logging is much less prominent here today than it was in the past. The remnants of the Rudy

Sawmill itself are nearly hidden in a dense forest. Despite the devastation that occurred a century or more ago, the forest has outlasted the timber industry.[1]

NOTE

1. Information on the Rudy, Erb, and Oaks families comes from tax records and the 1870 and 1880 census records consulted at the Huntingdon County Historical Society, property deeds researched in the Huntingdon County Courthouse, and J. Simpson Africa, *History of Huntingdon and Blair Counties, Pennsylvania* (Philadelphia: Louis H. Everts, 1883; reprint, Evansville, Ind.: Unigraphic, 1977). General information on sawmill operations and the logging industry in Pennsylvania comes from Thomas R. Cox, *The Lumberman's Frontier: Three Centuries of Land Use, Society, and Change in America's Forests* (Corvallis: Oregon State University Press, 2010), and Benjamin F. G. Kline Jr., *"Pitch Pine and Prop Timber": The Logging Railroads of South-Central Pennsylvania* (Strasburg, Pa.: Railroad Museum of Pennsylvania, 1999). Information on Penn State's logging practices in Stone Valley comes from Donald D. Stevenson, H. Arthur Meyer, and Ronald A. Bartoo, *Management Plan for Stone Valley Experimental Forest* (University Park: Pennsylvania State University, 1943). Information on the local iron industry comes from Nancy S. Shedd, *Huntingdon County, Pennsylvania: An Inventory of Historic Engineering and Industrial Sites* (Washington, D.C.: Department of the Interior, National Park Service, 1991). You can read more about the history of Shaver's Creek and Stone Valley in Jacy Marshall-McKelvey, *The History of Shaver's Creek*, forthcoming on the Shaver's Creek website.

Nothing Remains the Same

MARCIA BONTA (2015)

It's a humid, overcast July morning when my husband, Bruce, and I walk to the Rudy Sawmill site. Along the way, on the Lake Trail and later at Twin Bridges, we admire golden beds of fringed loosestrife and note that black raspberries are ripe. Across from a dilapidated sign saying "barn owl," we stop to marvel at a huge white oak tree. Through what seems to be an incredibly wet area, perhaps due to the almost unremitting rains of June, many more white oaks grow. This increasingly dwindling oak species seems to be thriving on this site.

When we reach the turnoff to the Sawmill Trail, we are amazed at how full Shaver's Creek is. As we head into the hemlock forest, we are greeted by the loud, explosive *pit-see* song of an Acadian flycatcher. Canada mayflowers blanket the forest floor, but we also see clusters of Indian pipes. The wet weather has been a boon to the ghostly-white Indian pipes. I've noticed that during dry summers they are scarce, and once, in the drought year 1988, none germinated on our property, but this year they have been plentiful.

Red-eyed vireos drone their incessant song loudly enough to be heard above the flowing creek. Large rhododendrons in glorious bloom hang over Shaver's Creek. Mushrooms in a kaleidoscope of colors—pink, dark purple, yellow, and white—light up the forest. *Teacher, teacher, teacher* calls an ovenbird as we arrive at the site of the old Rudy Sawmill. And the anticipated sun finally streams through gaps in the trees.

Nothing is left of the sawmill but a haphazard pile of rocks topped by a cluster of three small scarlet mushrooms. After standing in a patch of rattlesnake ferns and looking down at the site, I settle on a bed of moss beneath the hemlocks while Bruce climbs down to sit on a boulder beside Shaver's Creek. A breeze in the tops of the hemlocks sprinkles me with raindrops.

The Rudy Sawmill was a relatively small operation in the couple of decades it was a going concern until it ran out of lumber to mill. Years ago, back in 1972, Bruce's great-uncle Byron visited us at our newly purchased farm in Plummer's Hollow. Byron's Albertson family lived in northeastern Pennsylvania near Wilkes-Barre, but as he looked around our property, he told us that his father had operated a movable sawmill. Byron was certain that as a boy—and he was now seventy-two—he had accompanied his father on a logging expedition to our mountain and others in central Pennsylvania. That would have been the early twentieth century. Surely, by then, there wasn't much left to cut.

But there has always been the belief that trees are a renewable resource. If the Rudys thought of the future at all, they would have believed, as our neighbors do today, that the forest will grow back—as they continue to log their properties every twenty-five years so that it remains a young, brushy forest to feed the deer they hunt. They don't seem to notice or care that the quality of their forest has degraded, producing striped and red maple, black birch, and little else, because the large deer population they crave has eaten the oaks, black gum, basswood, tulip, and other tree species that sprout.

I'm not certain that the Rudys had the luxury of planning for the future of their offspring or their denuded landscape. It must have been difficult enough to survive in those days if you owned a small business and had a large family. Like humans everywhere, even those, like our neighbors, who already have more than enough, they had no interest in planning for future generations. And the trees did come back after their operation, but no doubt they were cut again, maybe by Bruce's great-uncle, since this forest is about a hundred years old. Or maybe the poor farms were still struggling along and no forest flourished until the farmers were bought out.

Now that this valley is treasured as a natural place, it may be allowed to transition into an old-growth forest. But wait. This forest is already dying a premature death. Not by the chainsaw but by an Asian immigrant—the hemlock woolly adelgid. Already I can see the cottony white masses on some of the needles and stems where the females shelter and lay their eggs. Will the trees be harvested after they die, or will they be allowed to rot in place, providing food for insects and other invertebrates?

And what will happen to Shaver's Creek? If the hemlocks die, as they have at the Hemlock Natural Area in Tuscarora State Forest, they will be replaced by black birch. Birch will not cast the dense shade that keeps the water cool for fish and the tiny aquatic organisms they eat. The hemlock needles that fall into the creek sustain a different and wider variety of macroinvertebrate species than streams lined with hardwoods can boast.

"Hemlocks," says Donald Eggen, forest health manager for Pennsylvania's Department of Conservation and Natural Resources, "are what we call a foundation species. That means it's the dominant life form in the habitat. Everything else is there because the hemlocks are there."[1]

The hemlocks' deep shade keeps out most other plants but provides shelter and warmth for more than 120 vertebrate species, including ninety species of birds. The last two cold winters have knocked back the adelgids— temperatures below zero Fahrenheit have been a respite for the hemlocks. And even though hemlocks have been killed from the Great Smoky Mountains up through the Appalachians to Pennsylvania, not all the hemlocks die in some places. Still, barring a natural predator of the woolly adelgids—and scientists have been studying possible Asian beetle species—this place will eventually transition into a hardwood forest.

But today I am enclosed in a green curtain only slightly pierced by hazy sunlight. A black-throated green warbler sings *trees, trees, beautiful trees*, and I can only agree. What a contrast this peaceful retreat is to what was once a noisy commercial enterprise.

As we take our leave, we hear the rattling call of a belted king-fisher. They probably have a nest dug back into the creek bank. Here I spot a patch of partridgeberry and there a cluster of Christmas ferns. Best of all, I find a few plants of striped wintergreen, although they have no buds or blossoms, so they must be only a year or two old. I've been watching as one striped wintergreen plant increased to nine inside our three-acre deer exclosure. It took several years for the oldest plants to produce flowers, and this July I counted three with nodding white waxy blossoms. Striped wintergreen (*Chimaphila maculata*), also known as spotted wintergreen, has evergreen leaves striped with white and would be a ground cover in some places if the deer didn't relish it.

A member of the Pyrola family, striped wintergreen is a close relative of pipsissewa, which I haven't seen since I was a child in the late 1940s, when the deer herd was sparser. My dad used to point it out to me during our outings in the hills of eastern Pennsylvania near Pottstown, where he had grown up.

Newcomb's Wildflower Guide calls striped wintergreen a plant of woodlands or bogs; the *Peterson Field Guide to Wildflowers* says it is found especially in uplands. Then there is the eccentric old *Wild Flowers of the Alleghanies* by Joseph E. Harned, who claims that it is usually found in deep pine forests.

But here it is in a deep hemlock forest, and in our exclosure it grows under a hardwood forest. How little we still know about the many wildflowers we name as we walk through field and forest. How little about what will be here in a hundred years.

Nature, despite our often rapist's approach to it, will survive in some form or another, but will humans? That, it seems to me, is the question for the twenty-first century, as we continue to live beyond the means of the earth to provide. But those who do, and I suspect small pockets will survive even a nuclear holocaust, extreme climate change, food and water shortages, and whatever else is thrown at them, may live more like the Rudys than the way we live today.

NOTE

1. Quoted in Lara Lutz, "Tiny Insect Toppling Region's Majestic Hemlocks," *Bay Journal*, June 9, 2015, http://www .bayjournal.com/article/tiny_insect _toppling_regions_majestic_hemlocks.

The Saw (Perpetual) Mill

JULIANNE LUTZ WARREN (OCTOBER 2015)

Tulip, maple, birch, beech . . . also oak and white pine, among others. A leaf fell behind my back. I quickly turned, wondering for an instant what animal I might glimpse. Here was an old hemlock cut, about twenty-two inches in diameter, and, of course, mossy. I sat again on a log, this log, though now with lunch already having filled my stomach. I looked around. It was as if a giant bagel had made a dense imprint on this very ground—a round center ringed by a trough.

I sat in that center for a while, listening. I returned two days later and did the same. Temperatures that second afternoon peaked at seventy-two degrees Fahrenheit. Among the birds chorusing at this site were red-breasted nuthatches (maybe white-breasted ones, too), a crow or two, and a downy woodpecker. Spare avian voices joined with the breezy percussion of those few still-falling leaves and the rolling water, reminding me that I was just upstream from the two bridges, on the same creek, a bit farther yet from the cliffs with their elemental mixtures of rushing drips and splashes. Here, a piece of the stream became part of a roundabout connecting two ends of an arcing dry-ground channel, surrounding me in its hub.

A circle in a circle, circling.

Jacy's "History of Shaver's Creek" says that four sons of farmer Jonas Rudy operated the sawmill here for just twenty-two years. The Rudys' mill was, by necessity or choice, a modest affair. Steam power was available, but this family used the older technology of a waterwheel. Its turning powered a saw to cut trees into small pieces. Moreover, the scale of this mill destined its output as building lumber rather than for burning into charcoal. The eighteenth-century discovery of iron ore in this area had led to intense logging for charcoal making through the following decades, answering the needs of smelting furnaces. By the time the Rudys got their mill up and running, many surrounding ones already had shut down. The burning appetite they had been feeding, within decades, had depleted timber stocks—

that is, the hunger for charcoal to produce iron to produce stoves to burn more wood, and also coal. Circles.

Not all wheels can be kept turning.

I got up and walked around the "bagel" trough surrounding me, stepping over fallen branches, walking between new growths of trees. The circumference is about two hundred paces. In accord with the modesty of the Rudys' mill, you might mistake this 150-year-old trace of the old "race" for weathered topography. The brothers had probably dug this relatively shallow ditch to divert the creek's flowing water to turn the bucketed wheel. I imagined I was water following the sluice.

I *am* water—mostly.

I circled, as in a traffic roundabout. I entered the trough, left, from upstream, flowed round through the forest, and returned, left, downstream into the creek—relieved to move on, freer than freedom—into the Juniata River into the Susquehanna River into the Chesapeake Bay into the Atlantic Ocean. Perhaps, along with helping carry sediment, I gave a fish breath now and again. Next, warmed by sunlight, I became rain. I helped grow a leaf, porcupine, and birdsong.

This wheel's perpetual turning means life.

The Chestnut Orchard

TRAILHEAD NOTE

From the Sawmill Site, your trek to the Chestnut Orchard involves first retracing your steps to the Twin Bridges. But rather than turning right across the creek, continue straight on the Lake Trail through low, often wet ground shaded by hemlocks. In a few hundred feet, a trail to the right would take you on a boardwalk through the swampy upper reaches of Lake Perez—more wetland than lake at this point. But save that boardwalk trail for another day and continue through the woods until you reach the open meadows of Stone Valley Recreation Area. The Lake Trail continues through tall pines in the meadow, along the lakeshore to the right and a row of cabins to the left. You can see the dam at the far southern end of the lake, but for now, turn left across Scare Pond Road and enter the woods on the Old Faithful Trail—maybe pausing to scratch a spearmint-scented twig from the yellow birch at the entrance to the trail. On Old Faithful, you find yourself in the cool of another hemlock forest, heading uphill a half mile or so along the thread of rill only a step or two across.

At the top of the ridge, turn right on the Mountain View Trail, following the trace of an old woods road until you come out to an intersection of dirt roads, Scare Pond and Hammond. And there, in the crook of the two roads, behind an eight-foot-high wire fence, stand rows of scrawny trees, where researchers are attempting to backcross American chestnuts with blight-resistant Chinese chestnuts. Their goal is to bring back a tree that was once dominant in eastern hardwood forests—or at least a simulation of the original chestnut, with just enough of the nonnative chestnut genes to provide resistance to the blight.

It's the fence, it seems, that draws the attention of the ecoreflectors at this spot. As admiring as they may be of the well-intentioned efforts of the researchers who have planted these rows of trees, the ecoreflectors are distinctly uncomfortable with the fence. It seems to suggest that we have taken the natural world captive, imprisoned the wild in a zoo or a jail cell. Or maybe it's that the aspiring chestnuts have been taken into some sort of protective custody. Whatever it is, that fence seems to say something about human relations with the natural world in our time.

Which Side Are You On?

MICHAEL P. BRANCH (2014)

My friend Ian Marshall, founder of the LTERP, has offered to lead me through the forest to the Chestnut Orchard site today. He and his son, Jacy, who is also a volunteer at Shaver's Creek, grab their day packs and walking sticks and head off down the paved road toward a break in the canopy, through which we enter a green tunnel into the woods. Before I can settle into much of a hiking rhythm, we come upon a huge eastern hemlock tree—one that does not look at all well. With some discernible heaviness in his voice, Ian explains that the tree is being killed by the hemlock woolly adelgid, and he bends the tip of a low-hanging branch up to show me its underside, where the adelgid's cottony egg sacks are thickly distributed. Next spring, the larvae will emerge from these sacks and proceed to spread hemlock death to other trees.

Hemlock woolly adelgid was introduced accidentally from Japan in the early 1950s, but its spread has accelerated in recent years, and now more than half of the eastern hemlock's natural range has been affected by what amounts to a pestilent form of biological contamination. Although the adelgid has been less destructive in the colder, northern half of the tree's range, the ecosystemic and phenological shifts associated with global warming could make even the northernmost hemlocks susceptible to the pest. While many of the hemlocks in the forest through which we're hiking today appear healthy, that could change quickly. One recent study grimly suggests that most of the hemlocks in this part of the range could be dead within a decade.

The painful term "anticipatory nostalgia" has been used to describe that odd, poignant feeling that strikes us when we look closely at something beautiful that we have reason to believe is about to vanish forever. This wounded feeling heightens our appreciation but also casts a pall over our enjoyment. It is an experiencing of the wound before the injury has occurred, a way of mourning the death of something that has yet to perish. In this sense, it brings the future into the present, death into life. The thrill of seeing the hemlocks in this forest is dampened for me as I wonder how many more LTERPreters will be able to share this experience. Perhaps some future visitor will write about having seen hemlocks only in photographs.

The prospect of this sort of catastrophic loss is hardly hypothetical in this forest, where as we hike toward a high ridge we identify ten-foot-tall American chestnuts. These are nothing more than chestnut suckers, small shoots of the once giant trees (up to ten feet in diameter) that were wiped out across their historical range by chestnut blight, a disease caused by an Asian bark fungus accidentally introduced during the early twentieth century. Within twenty years, the disease had killed several billion trees. Here in Pennsylvania, where a quarter to a third of the forest once consisted of chestnuts, the devastation was inconceivable. These suckers we see along the trail, which have no chance of surviving to maturity, are reminders of the ghost forest that is growing here—one consisting of giant, graceful, useful trees that are gone forever. Seeing these doomed shoots is a constant reminder of how real the threat to the eastern hemlock is. Will the hemlock forest also become a ghost forest?

Along the trail ahead of us, Jacy spots a black rat snake, one of the largest I've ever seen. We take a visual field mark on the location of its head and tail and then, once it has crawled away into the leaves and duff, use Ian's walking stick to take a measurement. We agree that this is a six-footer! I remember that this beautiful snake is not only an excellent climber and good swimmer but also a constrictor, suffocating its prey in the tightened coil of its lithe, shimmering body. In this sense, its species name, *Obsoleta obsoleta*, might be better applied to the squirrels, rabbits, and birds that are its prey than to the snake itself. Black rat snakes have on occasion even been known to vanquish the kinds of birds that you'd think would be its predators rather than its prey: daunting raptors like great horned owls and red-shouldered hawks. When not hibernating with timber rattlers and copperheads, these guys often climb trees and inhabit woodpecker holes, from which I imagine they have a spectacular view.

At last we crest a ridge and see before us something remarkable and strange: a second, smaller forest enclosed within a wire cage. This is the so-called Chestnut Orchard, where a variety of chestnut species are being experimented with in an attempt to develop a strain that will preserve the genetic integrity of the American chestnut while also being resistant to chestnut blight. Theoretically, this experiment could result in a new tree—or, more precisely, a new genetic variant of an old tree—that could survive to maturity, and thus might be replanted throughout the devastated American chestnut's historical range. It is a big dream to hang on such a small plot—a big idea to imagine that billions of vanished trees might someday be replaced with trees arising from these few acres of test specimens. But I also think of Gregor Mendel in his little patch of pea plants, making the humble observations that would alter our understanding of life itself. Long before Watson and Crick described the mechanism, the friar had intuited the process of hybridization and cross-fertilization that would profoundly change the human relationship to other organisms in the biosphere. A similar experiment is under way at this site.

Ian and Jacy eventually head back, leaving me to contemplate this strange place. I pace the perimeter fence like a caged animal, but on the outside looking in. Perhaps this plot is a kind of zoo, with its rare species well protected behind the tall fence through which we are to observe them. Or am I the animal behind the fence? I enter the test plot through a hatch in the fence and stroll the rows of trees in what now comes to seem like a chestnut garden—an orderly, well-tended, fence-encircled garden of trees. Not long after I enter the plot, though, I find myself looking back at the "real" forest that grows outside the fence. Now the Chestnut Orchard has come to feel a bit like a prison (are there surveillance cameras somewhere around here?), and increasingly I'm in the mood for a jailbreak. I climb back out the hatch and into the weeds growing alongside the dirt road. Orchard, forest, zoo, garden, prison. This place is hard to get a handle on.

I think my problem with this spot is making a clear determination about which side of the fence is inside and which is outside. John F. Kennedy once wrote, "Don't ever take a fence down until you know . . . why it was put up," an insight that applies to more than just fences around trees.[1] But I do have an urge to tear this fence down. Free the chestnuts! Island biogeography teaches us that habitat loss has left us with only scraps of ecosystems that once were whole—scraps that are often isolated and remote, scraps that now amount to little more than an archipelago of fragments. Putting up a fence doesn't change that, but it brings to mind that majestic ghost forest that now grows only in old photographs, in our imaginations, and in suckers that are born to die. This plot is a small, isolated piece of a larger story inscribed on manuscript pages that are now scattered by wind.

Perhaps understanding the meaning of this fence does not have to do with determining which side of it contains what is natural and which side contains what is artificial. In an era of anthropogenic global climate change and obscene biodiversity loss, maybe the lesson of this fence is that there no longer is an inside or outside. Although the fence gives me an uncomfortable feeling, it simply makes visible what would be true with or without it. The distinction between nature and our influence upon it was packed tightly into a crate that was stored deep within the hold of a ship that sailed long ago. In my imagination, the wide planks of that stout ship were hewn from the immense bole of an American chestnut.

NOTE

1. Hugh Rawson and Margaret Miner, eds., *The Oxford Dictionary of American Quotations*, 2nd ed. (New York: Oxford University Press, 2006), 201. The source is a 1945–46 personal notebook of John F. Kennedy, who attributes the line to G. K. Chesterton—though in truth Chesterton didn't say it so succinctly. Rather, in a longer passage in *The Thing* (1929), Chesterton talks about a law or institution as, metaphorically, a fence, and suggests that before reformers start tearing it down, they should first understand why it was put up. The passage explains a principle that has come to be known among legal scholars as "Chesterton's Fence" and among logicians as the "Fallacy of Chesterton's Fence" (the "fallacy" referring to those who would start tearing down a fence, law, institution, or policy without thinking through its reason for being there in the first place). As any Google search will show, many have since misattributed the statement to Robert Frost, probably the result of confusing Chesterton's fence with those mentioned in "Mending Wall," the ones that make good neighbors.

Reflections on Ecology from the Chestnut Grove

CAROLYN MAHAN (2014)

Monday, May 5
9:40–noon
0% cloud cover, 50–60° F, calm winds
Blue jay family (5)
Blooming pussy toes
Rue anemone, dandelion
Field sparrow
Great crested flycatcher
American redstart
Ovenbird
Black-capped chickadee
American crow
American goldfinch
Rufous-sided towhee
Raven
Red-tailed hawk
Tufted titmouse
Northern cardinal
Blue (azure) butterfly (.5")

Why am I here today, after some procrastination, for the first of my ecological reflections?

Well, the clear skies, strong sun, and semester's end combined to eliminate all excuses. The warblers are pouring back in from Central and South America and I want to note their arrival (welcome them?).

Why is the American Chestnut Experimental Plantation my first stop? I know why. My students and I have been involved in forest restoration at the Flight 93 Memorial for the past three years. As part of that restoration, we have been planting hybrid American chestnuts. This year, we planted a thousand American chestnuts that were 15/16 pure. These seedlings could be descendants of the American chestnut hybrids here in this enclosure at Shaver's Creek. (It is cool to find American chestnut leaves in the leaf litter after a hundred-year absence!)

American chestnuts were killed by a fungal blight in the 1920s. Prior to that, this species dominated the ridges of the mid-Appalachians. This past April, Stan Temple (from the Leopold Center at the University of Wisconsin–Madison) gave a talk at Penn State about the extinction of the passenger pigeon. The dominance of the passenger pigeon was related to the dominance of the chestnut because pigeons fed heavily on acorns and kept oak numbers low. That permitted the chestnut to dominate many areas within the range of passenger pigeons. They would move their roosting sites yearly to areas where the oaks were masting, and thus had a secure and concentrated supply of food. When the passenger pigeons were hunted to extinction, oaks could expand. Oak expansion really took off once the blight killed the competing chestnut. Now the suppression of fire and the expanding white-tailed deer population have resulted in oak decline and red maple expansion. Our forests keep changing.

So now forest management comes into play. The creation of a blight-resistant chestnut (via backcrossing with the Chinese chestnut), the limited use of prescribed fire, and an attempt to limit the deer herd may change our forests again.

Most celebrate the potential return of the chestnut—most environmentalists will herald its return. But isn't it just another example of a genetically modified organism, a dreaded GMO? Monsanto Corporation and our Department of Agriculture are vilified for developing GMOs—yet I am sitting mere yards from a GMO that is a beacon of hope for forest restoration. Stan Temple ended his talk by describing methods by which band-tailed pigeons could be used to foster "cloned" passenger pigeons. The passenger pigeon DNA could be provided via extraction from museum specimens. We caution about the ethics of cloning an animal—yet do not hear similar concerns expressed about these chestnuts. As a biologist, I am excited about the return of the American chestnut and hope someday we can do the same for the disappearing eastern hemlock (disappearing via hemlock woolly adelgid) and white ash (its decline due to emerald ash borer), but at the same time I am concerned and cautious about our use of biological tech to "fix" things.

The Chestnut Plantation

JOHN LANE (2016)

After we left the Dark Cliffy Spot, we walked along a very steep ridge on the Mountain View Trail. Near where the ridge levels out, we stopped to take pictures with a carved log statue of a man that maybe someone on a trail crew had created with a chainsaw out of a white pine log. David Gessner, one of the earlier LTERPreters, has always kidded me about the "old man" reading glasses dangling around my neck, so I put the glasses and my cap on the wood man and mugged away for the camera. It was a great moment of fellowship and humor among all of us on the hike, evoking two important aspects of nature recreation. Besides the fun we had, I also like to think of the fun the trail crew had, not dutifully clearing a log from the trail but creating a prime example of what Werner Herzog calls "the conquest of the useless." What use is that sculpture high on the Mountain View Trail? No use at all, except that it challenged the imagination of the one who carved it, and it created a place for those who pass to pause and marvel, to laugh, to shake their heads in wonder and delight.

Where the Mountain View Trail comes out at the Chestnut Plantation, I stopped and took in the view—a fence and the scrubby trees behind it. This, I could see, would be a hard reflection to get some intellectual purchase on—part tree stalag (to be fair, the fence is there to keep deer out, not the chestnuts in), part hard science research plot, part neglected science experiment. It might be fair, in the spirit of Ian Marshall's naming of the Dark Cliffy Spot, to call it, affectionately, "the weird treey (s)plot."

"The plantation" (could any southerner visit this place without putting scare quotes around that term, even though the word *plantation* has a much larger history and context than what southerners envision anytime we hear it?) was a three-acre experimental plot planted in 2003 by Xi Sigma Phi, the forestry honor fraternity, and the American Chestnut Society in an attempt to develop a disease-resistant American chestnut more than a century after the deadly blight wiped out billions of the trees.

We crawled through a clanging gate in the eight-foot-high deer fence and walked the rows of chestnuts. There were green, living trees, partly dead trees, and completely dead trees. I wished that some mad chainsaw artist would pass through the gate and get to work carving these snags into something whimsical—maybe wooden models of the very fungus that did in the original forest?

There were a few saplings in blue plastic tubes, suggesting the ongoing nature of the experiment, and my hope began to rise when I saw them. Maybe the results are sequestered somewhere in a forest researcher's computer that will provide the magic key to bringing back the species!

Some of the healthy trees, the Chinese variety with long, skinny, serrated leaves, had fruit—thorny green husks. Other specimens had the familiar wider serrated leaves of the American chestnut but no fruit that I could see. The profile of most of the trees was shrubby—more horizontal than vertical—and there wasn't much noble about the grove yet. None of Longfellow's "spreading chestnut trees" here.

I stopped amid the rows and scrambled for some couplets in my journal. Writing would give me, I thought, some lyrical purchase among the experimental rows, but what came out instead was doggerel:

Once a noble tree filled the view
Now planted are a scrubby few.

The Chinese cousin was invited in
To add their genes through familiar sin.

I closed my journal and we left the plot the way we came in, through the clanging gate. It was hard to make much sense out of whether the fraternity and the society had been successful or not, based on the trees growing in the plot, but I saluted their vision and commitment and wished them luck as I walked away.

Maybe I was tired when we explored the plot, as we had been hiking up and down the ridge for a couple of hours. Maybe one really needs to be refreshed and optimistic to respond properly to an endeavor as complex and hopeful as a large-scale restoration, and in particular to a Big Idea restoration like the return of the American chestnut to its former glory.

On the other side of the road, we stopped to look at the open view of the mountain across the valley (hence the name of the trail), and from that perspective I got my first glimpse of the "ridge and valley" topography I was nestled within at Shaver's Creek. There isn't this regularity to the geology I am familiar with in the Blue Ridge. The ridges and valleys aren't laid out in such straight lines five hundred miles south of here. I also wondered how different the hue and texture of the ridge might have been when covered with American chestnuts, and how thick that very forest floor would have been with fallen chestnuts a hundred years ago, maybe in the last autumn before the blight left the forest full of standing silver snags.

At the base of Josh's Chestnut Plantation interpretive sign, Justin uncovered a plastic box with the notes of a geocache inside. Ian and Justin read some of the recorded entries out loud, and Ian even read a couplet of poetry written by one of the visitors: "Nice view, / Though a bit of deer poo." Ah, I remind myself, in nature I am not the only one who wants to be a poet!

We ended our hike with a steep descent along the trail known as "Old Faithful." Along the way, Ian pointed out some chestnut sprouts, maybe four feet tall, and I became much more animated and reflective than I had been back up on the ridge at the Chestnut Plantation. Ian explained that the sprouts grow up out of the old stumps, full of expectation at becoming mature trees, and when they become tall enough for the bark to split, the deadly fungus that originally came from Asia gets in and kills them. How is it possible to maintain a truly optimistic spirit in the face of so many environmental screwups?

Earlier that day, before Ian arrived, I had been out back of the Environmental Center with naturalist Doug Wentzel when he showed a visitor a little brown bat roosting above the back door. I looked up and saw it tucked up in there. The visitor asked about the fungal disease that's killed so many of the North American cave-dwelling bats.

"I know it's sad," Doug said, "but there are good people at work to solve this problem."

This might become my mantra for restoration. Maybe it could be a sign to hang on the fence at the Chestnut Plantation:

The chestnut forests are gone.
We know this is sad.
But there are good people at work to solve the problem.

Almost Lost

KATIE FALLON (2016)

My mother is a retired children's librarian. She began reading to me when I was still in the womb; after, she filled my crib with books. She tells me that I could recite *The Tale of Peter Rabbit* by the time I was three and could read before kindergarten. It's no surprise that I first heard of a chestnut tree in a poem my mother read to me often:

> Under a spreading chestnut-tree
> The village smithy stands;
> The smith, a mighty man is he,
> With large and sinewy hands.[1]

Scenes filled with sensory details unfold—a muscled, sweaty man with long black hair, sparks flying from his anvil, swings a sledge-hammer from dawn until dusk, bending metal into horseshoes. He has several children, and they all go to church on Sundays; there, even though he's a large, rough man, the smith remembers his dead wife and cries. The poem is "The Village Blacksmith" by Henry Wadsworth Longfellow; I remember huddling next to my mother while she read it, wondering what "sinewy" meant, and wondering how a "spreading" tree would look. At that time—the early 1980s—I didn't know that nearly all of our chestnut trees were gone, or that the ones remaining would never grow tall enough for a blacksmith to "swing his heavy sledge" beneath their limbs.

According to the American Chestnut Foundation, this species of tree "reigned over 200 million acres of eastern woodlands from Maine to Florida . . . until succumbing to a lethal fungus infestation, known as the chestnut blight, during the first half of the 20th century. An estimated 4 billion American chestnuts, up to 1/4 of the hardwood tree population, grew within this range."[2] Folklore claims that a squirrel could climb into a chestnut tree in Maine and travel all the way to Georgia without ever touching the ground or a different species of tree. But in 2016, just a few wild, mature individuals can be found in Appalachia; young chestnut trees still spring near old stumps but succumb to the blight before maturing.

I walked along the tall fence of Penn State University's Chestnut Plantation and blinked away the spring rain. New leaves filled the branches of many of the trees before me, and a few even sported burrs—large seedpods covered in spikes. Inside the burrs gleamed smooth, shiny chestnuts, subject of song and story, once food for cattle, hogs, and humans—roasted on an open fire, of course, for the last. A sign posted near the fence said that this plot had been planted with chestnut seedlings in 2003, and that "data collected from this chestnut planting will be used to help develop disease resistant American Chestnuts." The American Chestnut Foundation and research partners across the continent had developed a tree that was, genetically, 15/16 American chestnut and 1/16 Chinese chestnut. I wondered if some of the trees here were these hybrids, crossed in the hope that the trees would "act" like American chestnuts while retaining the Chinese chestnut's resistance to the blight. The hybrids offered the hope that one day the American chestnut—or at least a tree that was *almost* an American chestnut—would return to the eastern United States.

The chestnut trees inside the wire fence weren't tall—the tallest was perhaps fifteen feet and most were shorter than that—and grew next to colored or numbered stakes. The leaves were shiny, their edges toothed like saw blades. The leaves drooped in clusters from the branches, perhaps weighed down by the rain. While some of the trees were thin, many reminded me of fat Christmas trees—longer branches on the bottom, and the branches shortening and shortening as they moved up the trunk, giving an almost triangular impression of the tree as a whole. But some defied this shape and instead resembled a child's drawing of a tree—a very short trunk with a round, cotton-ball-shaped blob upon it.

In his poem "Mending Wall," Robert Frost famously wrote, "Something there is that doesn't love a wall, / That wants it down," but his neighbor insists, "Good fences make good neighbors."[3] The fence around the Chestnut Plantation is here in part to keep out white-tailed deer. I'm sure it's necessary, and while the fence makes the deer "good neighbors" to the young (and probably expensive) experimental chestnut trees, I am one of the "somethings" that doesn't love a wall. I wanted to touch the young chestnut trees, to feel the smoothness of the shiny leaves. I noticed that the bottom branches of many of the trees grew low to the ground—in fact, almost parallel to the ground, ladder rungs, maybe, for a gentle foot. I considered scaling the fence and trying my luck at climbing one of the larger trees, although I'm not sure the thin branches would have held me. Perhaps a larger specimen—like the "spreading chestnut tree" that shaded the village blacksmith—would have invited climbing. I bet a person could have gotten lost in the branches of a tree like that. Not me, though. Those days are gone. Those trees are gone.

Standing at the fence, staring in at the rows of young chestnut trees, I felt like I was visiting a zoo. The lives that populated the exhibit weren't wild, necessarily, but they weren't domesticated either. Of course, these trees didn't pace like caged lions or bat beach balls around like captive bears, but they were similar. Still here, but diminished. Fenced. Modified. What do the trees know? They breathe, they sway, they push energy into catkins and burrs. You hear about wild, remnant chestnut trees occasionally, the way you sometimes hear about ivory-billed woodpecker or eastern cougar sightings. Once, at a festival dedicated to American chestnuts in Rowlesburg, West Virginia, I'd been lamenting the loss of this species when a gray-haired man, bent and thin with arms like gnarled branches, pulled me aside. "There are some still out there," he said, almost whispering. "Big ones. They're not gone."

I don't know if I believe him, but I enjoy picturing a forest filled with American chestnut trees, the trunks shooting skyward as the branches spread, yellow-white catkins exploding from the twigs. The burrs, those spiky green golf balls, would swell on the trees before dropping and cracking open, spilling their seeds. Deer would eat them, and turkeys and bears. The passenger pigeon, extinct by 1914 but perhaps once the most numerous bird on the planet, depended on American chestnuts for food. Maybe, in a hundred years, scientific advances will have saved not only the American chestnut but will have brought back the passenger pigeon as well. I hope that in a hundred years there will be no need for this fence, no need for chestnut plantations, because we will have solved the blight. And wild trees will flourish. Perhaps villagers will be able to gather beneath the trees again as they spread across the mountains, reclaiming Appalachia's soil with their roots. Perhaps children will swing their legs up and over the low branches and pull themselves higher and higher, until they are lost among the leaves of a tree that once was almost lost itself.

NOTES

1. Henry Wadsworth Longfellow, "The Village Blacksmith," http://www .hwlongfellow.org/poems_poem .php?pid=38.

2. American Chestnut Foundation, http:// www.acf.org.

3. Robert Frost, "Mending Wall," in *The Poetry of Robert Frost: The Collected Poems, Complete and Unabridged*, edited by Edward Connery Lathem (New York: Henry Holt, 1969), 33.

The Dark Cliffy Spot

And now we come to the most remote and out-of-the-way of the ecological reflections sites: the Dark Cliffy Spot. To get here from the Chestnut Orchard, you follow the Mountain View Trail as it first parallels Scare Pond Road, heading downhill. But in a half mile or so, the trail arcs above an open, sandy slope and turns left along a ridgeline, following it for more than a mile before descending to join the Shaver's Creek Trail, with the creek on the other side of the trail. You make a sharp left and cross a boggy meadow and then a bridge across an unnamed tributary of Shaver's Creek. After the bridge, turn left again on the Woods Route, following the tributary upstream. Where the trail comes closest to the stream, there's a lovely mini-canyon with steep rock walls above small, riffling pools—that's the original Dark Cliffy Spot (see Mike Branch's essay on the naming history of the site). But keep going, along the stream, following it around a sweeping left turn, until you see a bigger wall of rock across the stream—and yes, as Mike points out, compared to the first spot, this one is darker and not just cliffier but actually a cliff, a dramatic sheer wall with a large hemlock somewhat miraculously seeming to grow out of the side of the rock and bending upward. Looking up the cliff from the streambank, a breath-venting "wow" is the first word most people utter in response to the place.

It's that "wow" factor that encapsulates what happens here, it seems, for our LTERPreters, for the first thing "wow" does is take your attention away from your interior space to something outside the self—and bigger than the self. This is of course contrary to the image of the navel-gazing, solipsistic, spiritually questing nature writer, but this is one of the most valuable things the natural world does for us. It's a useful reminder, in these days when our kind seems

to dwell ever more exclusively on the peculiar doings of our own species, of the drama inherent in the more-than-human world. But the
connections we make in an excursion to the woods are not just to the
natural world; very often, when the experience is shared, the connections are made with one another. And when the excursion happens
in a memorable piece of landscape, the recollected experiences get
hitched up with the landmark, which becomes a geographical or geological mnemonic, not just an aid to memory but a container for it.
The thing that has surprised me the most in the first decade of the
Ecological Reflections Project is the web of conversation and storytelling that has passed back and forth among the LTERPreters. They
are in dialogue not just with the land but also with one another,
responding to what others have perceived at the same spot. Of all
the ecoreflection sites, the Dark Cliffy Spot may be the one that least
reminds us of the way natural places are preserved through human
mediation. At other sites, we can see the bars of cages where hawks
reside, or a fence that keeps deer out of an orchard, or mown fields
in a bluebird meadow—but even here, where human agency is not
so readily apparent, the threads of stories weave our human lives into
the warp and woof of the wild.

Ironically, this site that lies farthest off the beaten path also seems
to have inspired the most conviviality during the visits when we lead
LTERPreters on the grand tour of the sites. Maybe we're all giddy
with relief after the sweat-busting hike to get here, but this site seems
to inspire laughter and storytelling, mostly about the experiences of
those who have come before. And in the written responses to the
place, the ongoing conversation is evident not just in pieces like Mike
Branch's satirical account of the naming process but in David Taylor's
song about this spot. After all, a song is meant to be shared, both in
the making and in the hearing. And I note that Carolyn Mahan came
here in the company of her daughter, Clare, who gets the last word
or two regarding the various meanings of the place. Maybe what
inspires the sense of human connection at the Dark Cliffy Spot has
something to do with the signs that Carolyn mentions of a healthy
biological community here—something we all sense and respond to
with high spirits. Or maybe it's the power of wow.

The Dark Cliffy Place

A Fiction Fragment in Imitation of Cormac McCarthy

DAVID GESSNER (2012)

Stitler assessed this place he had found himself in with one greedy glance. The moss wall seemed to sweat and blocked out what little light there was. He licked at his wound like some sort of deranged cat and then nodded to himself as if he had come to some fine hotel for the night, a place that would meet all his needs.

Which it did in its way. He found sphagnum to rub in the wound and had spied huckleberries back down the serpentine path. Did the little creek hold crayfish for dinner? He would find out soon. On his way in he had passed a mill, and the place was spotted with houses, but something told him that this was the kind of place they would leave alone. He decided, for the first time in days, to risk a small fire. A reward for making it this far.

Cleanliness was not something that had had much priority in him for a while, but he decided to wander back to where he'd seen the hole to clean himself and the large gash in his right arm. He dipped his face in first, but gradually submerged the rest of himself. It was a baptism of sorts, though he knew it was the opposite of being born he was heading toward.

A part of him felt like simply stripping off his clothes and floating on his back, waiting for them to catch up with him. There had never been much chance of outrunning men on horseback anyway, though crimped-up places like this one helped. He had always been good at getting lost, and this was a lost sort of place.

When he got back to the spot, a bunch of crows had landed near his sack. Not big enough to be a murder—a mugging, maybe. He swore and charged and they were gone, complaining. He waded over to the cliff base and tore out a handful of liverwort, mixing it with the fiddleheads and mint he'd scooped up earlier and grazed. He decided he lacked the ambition for fishing, and noted that the gnawing hunger in his stomach was gone, which could be either a good sign or a bad one.

The pain in his arm, however, had gone nowhere. With his good arm, his left, Stitler searched for wood that was not soaked through. He managed to raise a smoky fire just about the time the last of the light shafts disappeared. He grazed a little more, spit it out, tasting something iron in his mouth.

As the dark fell, the fire threw a phantom show of light and shadows on the cliff wall. The shapes reached and leaped along with their creator. Dolls or puppets and then dragons and trolls, like some show from China. The shapes made him doubt the wisdom of choosing this place to stop. They seemed to have gotten inside him, moving around and spreading the pain from arm to chest. It gave him in turn a certain phantomish turn of mind. He heard the whirring of wings. The crows were back, and this time he couldn't get his voice to work or arms to wave.

He lay on his back and stared at the wall. He knew it was time to feed the fire but he had no will, or body, to do it. He doubted his choice of stopping here once again. Since his eyes were the only things about him that seemed to work, he turned them toward the mossy wall. The shadows grew taller as the fire died. He had a sudden fantasy that in the morning he would be his younger, stronger self, and he would clamber up that wall, his thin, strong fingers finding cracks, pulling himself up like a monkey.

But then even his fantasy turned sour. He fell from the rocks back into the creek, and when his pursuers finally found him he was there, on his back, arms spread out like a starfish.

Which wasn't so different from how he was feeling now. Like something that same moss might soon cover. He should get up and poke the fire, but instead he just lay there still. He had never been a churchgoer, laughing at it all even as a child. And he wasn't sure that he was ready, a scrawny, undersized Jesus, to sacrifice the one mean life he had known. But there didn't seem to be any choice in it.

About the time the shadows died on the wall, Stitler closed his eyes. A strange thought entered his mind, something about wading across the creek and planting a kiss on the moss. That would be his last thought. The pain was gone, which was good. He heard the creek and the crows. Then he felt his body shudder and slump, and he experienced a feeling that he might have described, if he still had words, as a sinking, a decaying down into the forest floor.

Song for the Unnamed Creek

DAVID TAYLOR (2013)

TALKING VERSE 1

Over on Mountain View Trail, there's a creek without a name. In Pennsylvania, that's not saying much—there's a creek flowing one way or another every time a cloud sniffles. But this one is special to me. I was hiking down the trail on a warm August day, sweating and dreary. Just about then the creek offered up a swimming hole, so I dropped my skivvies, donned my Tevas, and lay down right in the middle of it. There's nothing like 100 percent humidity to cure the discomfort of humidity. It's a bit overused to say I was immersed or baptized in the stream, but as I lay there, I just tried to see it.

CHORUS

No names are your waters; no sounds are your stone.
The poets' lines fail your calm, their odes are not your own.
I wish I had fierce, live words to reflect your beauty clear.
I'm not the one to name you, but I have to sing you're here.

TALKING VERSE 2

"Every word was once a poem. Every new relation is a new word," Emerson says. And I'm here in this nameless creek in a new relation. Knowing that this creek is in the timeless dance hall of the earth. I'm listening to the sound of eons—rock and water greeting each other and dancing and dancing, turning and dipping and holding on in cadences fast and slow. One leads and sometimes the other, a small ripple or a fall their curtseys, thank-yous, goodbyes and hellos. And I'm wanting to say to them how beautifully they twirl, the slight blue wiggly line on the map, the fish soaring like speckled or striped specters in mirror pools, three different kinds of ferns fixed to the slick, dark rock, and hemlock roots like fingers reaching into the streambank. How do I introduce myself? Say howdy? Say thanks? Say this place, this big turtleback home, the swaying pines and firefly stars are all the more there because of you, creek without a name. I have no words, no language that makes a river into an ear, or a human into running water. But if I don't say something, my life is without honor, my words and songs without weight. So I'll sing out! And let the words and sounds drift down the creek and over the ripples and pools, mixing and fading and making a relation I might someday understand.

CHORUS

No names are your waters; no sounds are your stone.
The poets' lines fail your calm, their odes are not your own.
I wish I had fierce, live words to reflect your beauty clear.
I'm not the one to name you, but I have to sing you're here.

TALKING VERSE 3

So here's to the new word, the new poem, the relation I am trying to make to you, nameless creek, something which I can't speak, write, or fully understand. Hell, even this song couldn't figure out a normal verse or melody to express itself. But maybe this is as it should be, because something typical just wouldn't be enough.

CHORUS

No names are your waters; no sounds are your stone.
The poets' lines fail your calm, their odes are not your own.
I wish I had fierce, live words to reflect your beauty clear.
I'm not the one to name you, but I have to sing you're here.[1]

NOTE

1. You can hear an audio recording of David singing this song, along with his photographs of the unnamed stream running through the Dark Cliffy Spot, at the Shaver's Creek website for the "Creek Journals," http://www.shaverscreek.org/about-us/initiatives/long-term-ecological-reflections-project/site-4/.

Naming a Place, Placing a Name

MICHAEL P. BRANCH (2014)

Where I live, at six thousand feet in the Great Basin Desert, virtually no natural features are named on USGS maps. The largest mountains have official names, but numberless canyons, hills, playas, and ridges do not. Each year I walk more than twelve hundred miles within a ten-mile radius of my home, an experiment in bioregional awareness that I have performed unfailingly for the past eight years. Over that much time and distance—that many hours and miles—it just makes sense to be able to tell your family where you're headed. I never sat down with a map and started naming places. Instead, the names grew organically over time and were linked to my experiences in those places. "Moonrise" is what I call the hill closest to our house, because it is an excellent spot from which to watch the moon levitate above the desert hills on summer nights. "Cornice Canyon" is named for the crested brow of windswept snow that develops atop its summit ridge in winter. For every Cornice Canyon there are a dozen other places that, through naming, I have also added to my personal cartography of that high desert landscape. These names express and mediate my relationship to place in meaningful ways.

In my meditations as an LTERPreter, I have often reflected on the names of the sites I have been invited to visit. But it is the Dark Cliffy Spot that I find most problematic, and I'd like to add right away that my friend Ian Marshall, who dreamed up the LTERP program, is personally responsible for this terrible name. I will of course take this up with him, but why should I do so only in conversation around the campfire when I can ridicule him here in my LTERP ruminations, where for the next century visitors to Shaver's Creek might join me in mocking Ian for his poor judgment?

Let's begin with the least intellectual formulation of the inquiry I propose: *What in the hell kind of name is "Dark Cliffy Spot"?* This isn't even a name, really, it is a description—and not even a good one. Why don't we just call central Pennsylvania "Green Hilly Spot" or Yosemite "Sheer Rocky Spot"? Maybe Ian would prefer it if I dropped his given name and started referring to him as "Tall, Guitar-Playing White Guy." *Dark Cliffy Spot?* The problems with this awful name are legion. To begin with, every place is dark at night, so this isn't a terribly bright way to distinguish a landscape feature. How would you find a dark spot at night? Just don't visit the Dark Cliffy Spot with a flashlight. You'll ruin everything!

Worse yet, "Cliffy" sounds like a noncommittal way to identify a cliff, as if the namer (in this case Ian himself) were hedging his bets in case some Nevadan who hangs out in Yosemite were to come to Shaver's Creek and say something like, "Dude, you call *that* a cliff?" Then, presumably, Ian could reply, defensively, "Look, I didn't say it *was* a cliff, I said it was *cliffy*." Even "clifflike" would have been better, because it would have the dual advantage of being a more transparent and thus more honest form of hedging, and would also sound less like the name of a guy from Connecticut who likes to play golf. (Can't you just hear it? "Hey, Cliffy, did you get us a tee time?") Or, if you're going to insult the cliff anyway, you might as well call it "cliffish." It all amounts to the same thing: "cliffy" conveys instantly that the feature I am about to experience is NOT A CLIFF! "Cliffy" is a cowardly moniker, one designed to lower my expectations. Next time I review a book Ian has written I'll be sure to characterize his writing as "creativish."

Having established that "dark" and "cliffy" were bad calls, we must now reckon with "spot." What is a spot? Something you do to a football. Something you get on your pants when you spill red wine. Something you name a dog. Something this dog leaves when it takes a leak on your neighbor's lawn. And in terms of locating this place, "spot" sounds oddly precise. The cliff is only "cliffy," but suddenly we are again in a world of certainty, where X marks THE spot? But which spot did Ian have in mind? And there's the still larger problem that "dark" and "cliffy" might be understood to describe the "cliff," or they might be thought to describe the "spot," which is itself entirely ambiguous in any case. In short, Ian's name for this place is as imprecise and spineless as a name could possibly be.

Now allow me to reveal the real scandal of this ridiculous name. The Dark Cliffy Spot is . . . wait for it . . . *not* the actual spot of the original dark cliff that was intended to be one of the LTERP sites. It turns out that while looking for Ian's Dark Cliffy Spot, a pair of Shaver's

Creek naturalists walked right past it. Little surprise, since it was daytime, the place has no cliff, and the spot is unmarked—though with these notable exceptions Ian's name was a model of precision. No, these skilled, trained, attentive naturalists weren't even close to being dumb enough to find the spot Ian had picked, and instead hoofed right by it and discovered an entirely different spot that is much darker, and is not only cliffier but in fact actually has a cliff. Guided by Ian's singularly unhelpful name for the place (and perhaps also by Momus, the Greek god of irony), these explorers failed to find the spot his name denoted and instead discovered a spot that is in fact a much better match with the name.

Now Ian had a problem. He hiked in there to check it out for himself and could see immediately that Dark Cliffy Spot #2 absolutely kicked the ass of Dark Cliffy Spot #1. In fact, in a moment of weakness he may even have craned his neck up at the impressive relief of this newly discovered cliff and been chagrined that he had ever used the word "cliffy." The somewhat rocky creek cutbank at Original Dark Cliffy Spot wasn't even a cliff—an insecurity his crappy name for it had from the start betrayed. But here at New and Improved Dark Cliffy Spot, calling this impressive vertical rock wall "cliffy" made as much sense as calling Bach and Beethoven "composeryish." What, then, should Ian do? He could stick to his convictions and continue to celebrate the less dramatic but also lovely Dark Cliffy Spot #1. Or he could adopt the new and more dramatic spot and rename it in a more descriptive and accurate way—something like "Tall Shady Cliff," let's say. Or he might do something innovative, like link the two spots together into one, as he did at the "Twin Bridges" site. Any of these would have been a logical solution to a very real problem. But what did Ian do instead? He did that thing that humans always do: embraced the better cliff, refused against reason to give up the old name, and just hoped everybody would forget about it. But the LTERP is about remembering the past and projecting the future, and so as an LTERPreter I have felt compelled to document for posterity how this lame name and its misplaced site came into use. If in the future one of you reading this hikes farther up the creek and finds an even better cliff, I suggest that you name it "Darkest Cliffiest Place." But if you do, keep watching over your shoulder. Can you be certain there's not an even darker, cliffier spot yet farther upstream?

Despite the name debacle surrounding it, the Darker Cliffier Spot is remarkably beautiful, and I feel as if I could sit here all day long. The cliff itself (and it *is* a cliff) is impressive: quite sheer, perhaps forty feet tall, leaning by turns away from and into the creek's airspace, bearded with moss. It is a legit cliff by any reasonable standard—the El Capitan of Shaver's Creek! At its base is an artistic jumble of angular stones, especially noticeable because the creek bed immediately upstream and downstream from this spot contains no large rocks at all. The stones in this haphazard pile are not worn to rounded edges, like trundled river cobble, but are instead blockish squares and rectangles that appear to have fallen from the face of the cliff. A number of trees, aspiring to become metaphors for the tenacity of life, grow straight out of the face of the rock. There are maple, beech, and oak saplings, as well as the star of the show, a large hemlock whose curving trunk and roots are grasping the rock and apparently penetrating it as well.

Why are certain landscape features so magnetic? Why, in the vast woods, does this spot hold so much attractive power? Perhaps it is something about diversity in aesthetic perception—the way we welcome change and surprise as we move through a landscape. In the miles of woods I have walked in the past few days, I have seen nothing remotely like this spot, and that in itself gives it monumental status. Others have apparently felt the same attraction. I find a very old fire ring nearby, and then, partially hidden in the leaves, a square of rocks three feet long on each side, a formation whose purpose eludes me.

I sit down on a rotting log facing the cliff. It is damp beneath me, and surprisingly soft. I notice on the log two showy growths— mushrooms, I suppose. One is a shield formation in the shape of a scallop, though with a narrower base than the shell would have and with a corrugated texture that makes it look a bit like tree bark. It is as large as my hand and tinted a lovely purplish red. Not far from it is a weird, phallic growth that is bright orange at its base, tapering to yellow as it rises, and creamy white at its flared top.

The name fiasco makes me think about the words we use in association with the LTERP: Bridge, Spot, Center, Trail, Site, Place. Each is a noun, of course, because it denotes a location, but each is also a verb (or a homophone of one) that implies action. I come to

Shaver's Creek *trailing* the desert along with me, but while here I try to *bridge* West and East by becoming *centered*—by *placing* a thought or memory, by hoping for the chance to *sight* or *spot* that pileated woodpecker. I think, too, of how much of our natural vocabulary emerges from the primacy of the visual sense. While we sometimes express understanding by saying "I *hear* you," more commonly we say, "I *see* what you mean." Darker Cliffier Spot is visually stunning. It makes you want to look and never stop looking. Where exactly did those rock blocks fall from? How did that big hemlock manage to survive in that impossible situation? Is that a shard of sunlight piercing the clouds in the deep forest that floats above the cliff?

I sit long enough to allow my mind to wander toward other ways of knowing place. What if instead of looking at this place I felt or smelled it? I decide to take off my boots and socks and wade through the little stream, which I could easily have rock hopped instead. What is it about having bare feet in cold, running water that clears the mind? I shuffle gingerly through the creek to the cliff, where I run my hands slowly across its face. When I close my eyes, I am better able to discern the fine texture of the moss, the hieroglyphic sensation of the rock. I concentrate on how this place feels on my skin: it is dank here, noticeably cooler than it was on the trail. I keep my eyes and mouth closed and breathe in deeply through my nose. I pick up a rich whiff of things growing and rotting, rotting and growing.

Now it is time to experience the soundscape of this interesting place. Of course the creek has been babbling all along (*babbling* is an insult that might be listed along with *cliffy*; I suspect we describe brooks as *babbling* only because we are too ignorant to comprehend what they're communicating). But now I want to *listen* to the creek rather than simply hear it. I rise from the old log, climb over to its forest side, and resume my sitting position, now facing the woods instead of the cliff. I take a last look at the curtain of green before shutting my eyes again. At first I hear nothing more than the same creek I've heard since I arrived here. Birdsong echoes in the canopy: the surge and lilt of a cardinal's call, the quieter notes of the phoebe, several others that I am not yet able to name. Then the creek again, just as before, only now I hear more resonance and sustain and amplification, and I realize how much of the sound of the stream is coming not from water but from rock. The height of the cliff and the curvature of its face function as a natural amphitheater for the creek's sonic performance.

I hear the birds again, and now also insects humming in the distance. Is that the soughing of a slight breeze stirring in the treetops? Focusing once again on the sound of water, for the first time I am able to hear what makes this spot so acoustically beautiful. There are two distinct sounds forming a single sound, just as the Twin Bridges might be seen as a single, two-part bridge that crosses Shaver's Creek. I now hear what I was unable to notice with my eyes: the jumble of rocks is in fact two separate jumbles, close together but absolutely distinct from each other. The upper mass of rocks creates a riffle in which the falling water strikes with a deep sound—not booming, but easily discernable as a bass (and base) note. The lower riffle has a distinctly higher pitch, as the moving water strikes further up the register in a clear treble note. I focus first on the bass, picking out its sound and mixing the treble down on the soundboard of my attention; then I reverse the process, pulling the bass down and heightening my awareness of the treble tinkling from the lower riffle.

Having performed this exercise in selective attention a number of times, I am better able to recognize the strands of sound that are braided together in the creek's song. To conclude this experiment in perception, I now focus on listening to the two sounds together. When I do, it brings a smile to my face. It is a goofy thing, this grinning alone in nature. I enjoy it whenever it happens. And mine is a smile of recognition, because at last I hear it with perfect clarity: the bass and treble riffles are harmonizing! Had I strutted up to the creek, reached for my pens, and blazed away at this place, I might have fired off tropes of harmony, as nature writers so often do. But I am smiling because the harmony I have discovered here is not metaphorical but literal. Come to this place and listen for yourself, and you will hear what I mean. Bass and treble, pitched together, harmonized, amplified, the reflected notes blended, shaped, and sustained by the graceful curvature of the cliff. This is not a metaphor for music. This *is* music.

Reflections on Ecology at the Dark Cliffy Spot

CAROLYN MAHAN (2014)

August 8

Sunny, 70° F, breezy

I brought my twelve-year-old daughter, Clare, with me today. She is looking for creatures in the stream. It is a quiet late summer day. Not one bird is singing but I did hear a blue jay call earlier.

This is a tributary of Shaver's Creek, a native brook trout stream. Brook trout are Pennsylvania's only native trout and our state fish. Although called a trout, they are actually a char and are related to Arctic char—a fish of the far North. Brook trout are declining throughout the Appalachians because of climate change (they need cool water), acid rain, and competition from introduced brown and rainbow trout. Also, our state tree, the eastern hemlock, is being wiped out by a nonnative insect, the woolly adelgid. The hemlock provides shade to these mountain brook trout streams, keeping waters cool in the summer.

Here, the darkness of the Dark Cliffy Spot is caused by the shade of hemlocks. I notice that the canopy of this hemlock stand is thinning—indicating that the hemlock woolly adelgid is here. Maybe in ten years this will just be the "cliffy spot."

Jewelweed, Pennsylvania smartweed, New England asters, and snakeroot are blooming in the understory. A few patches of wood sorrel—which always reminds me of the Pacific Northwest's old-growth forests—are also present under these hemlocks.

Clare was unable to catch any creatures in her net. She says the water is too cloudy to make a good capture attempt. It has been an unusually wet summer, and the stream is deeper and muddier than would be expected in August. However, she reports that she saw three water striders and two crayfish. The crayfish were "small and brown," which tells me they were probably in the genus *Cambarus*. These native crayfish are declining rapidly in Appalachian streams and have disappeared from many, replaced by larger, aggressive non-native crayfish in the genus *Orconectes*. The rusty crayfish, native to the central United States, is the most prevalent nonnative crayfish in Pennsylvania. It has been introduced to our streams by fishermen and -women who use them as bait. Crayfish are an important food source to many fish, herons, and riparian mammals (raccoons, mink)—but the large rusty crayfish may be responsible for the decline of native macroinvertebrates.

Okay, some good news—Clare just hiked to the top of a nearby hill and reports many large trees mixed with snags with lots of holes in them. These holes are the feeding holes of pileated woodpeckers, and the hairy woodpecker that I just heard suggests that there is a healthy community of snags and insects for these birds. Recent research found that a diverse assemblage of woodpeckers indicates an area of healthy forest with associated high biodiversity. So there are signs that this forest along Shaver's Creek is hanging in there—for now. It may continue to do so if our winters are cold enough (like last year's) to keep populations of hemlock woolly adelgid in check.

The trifecta of ravine trees is present here—yellow birch, American beech, and eastern hemlock—the three sisters of Allegheny ravines. All grow well in moist, low-light conditions, and they can grow on steep slopes with shallow soils because they are not deep-rooted trees.

"Steep," "muddy," "cool," "breezy," "rocky," "burbling stream," and "rustling" are Clare's descriptions of the place today.

The Bluebird Trail

Here comes the longest stretch of our daylong hike together, moving from the Dark Cliffy Spot situated past the southeastern corner of Lake Perez and all the way out to the Bluebird Meadow northwest of the lake. Retrace your steps to the Shaver's Creek Trail, and this time keep on the trail as it travels above the creek, past the turnoff to the Mountain View Trail on the right, then past the Spearmint Trail on the left, proceeding gently but steadily uphill through a forest of pine and hemlock. Shaver's Creek here, below the dam, is sizeable and enticing—if it's a hot day, feel free to go dip your feet or more in one of the pools where the creek bends and slows. Back on the trail, when it hits Scare Pond Road at a hairpin turn on its way up the ridge, take the path cutting through the woods on the left. You will come out in the Stone Valley Recreation Area meadow by a climbing wall and picnic pavilion. Across Lake Perez you can see the Civil Engineering Lodge and a boathouse, and even the traces of an old road that passed through the shallow swale that is now underwater. Turn left again on the Lake Trail, then right across the top of the dam at the head of Lake Perez. After crossing the dam, the trail heads uphill, away from the lake. You'll cross the West Entrance Road, then walk through a stand of pines, then hardwoods, and through a power-line cut. When the trail winds back down toward the lake, you'll bend left. The Lake Trail soon cuts right across a bridge on its way back to the Environmental Center, but you'll stay straight on the grassy footbed of the Bluebird Trail. At the stone remains of the old Mumma homestead, the trail curves right and across the foot of the meadow, then up its eastern edge before reentering woods at the top of the hill. Walk past the first open spot looking south down the meadow, past a pine on the left, till you get to a spot looking west over a smaller patch of the Bluebird Meadow.

This is a spot in flux, or interrupted in flux, a piece of forest succession artificially stalled in midprocess. As Scott Weidensaul describes it, this peaceful setting is the battleground for the contending forces of forest and field, native species and exotics, stasis and change. Perhaps that state of in-between-ness accounts for the fact that two of the ecoreflectors here, John Lane and I, end up blending the different literary forms of prose and poetry. But all the writers here seem intensely conscious of both the inescapable human presence—evident in the sounds of cars and chainsaws, in foundation ruins, climate change, and mown meadows that seek to preserve bluebird habitat—and the riot of activity from other living things thriving here—birds, insects, snakes, shrubs, and trees. The ecoreflections here are about the unchanging and the ever-changing dualities of the natural world—and the great question of how human influence, inescapably entwined in all of it, should play its part.

Battleground

SCOTT WEIDENSAUL (2006)

For all the other locations in this Ecological Reflections Project, I was shown to a particular spot, or asked to write about a general area, like the Lake Trail or out on Perez Lake itself. But here along the Bluebird Trail, I was given the pioneer's right of first choice—told that I was welcome to plant my flag anywhere that caught my fancy along the path, and that would remain the reflection point in perpetuity.

Well, now . . . like a homesteader weighing his options, I wander back and forth, up one hillock and down the next. I spend an hour here, half an hour there, watching the world go by, looking for some augury that will tell me I've arrived at The Spot. But the universe is mute, so I finally make my choice based on the simple pleasure of sitting in the first little meadow north of the Environmental Center, just above a short, steep hill falling to the stream. (Having come from the opposite direction, it was actually the last of a series of small openings and fields through which I'd passed, all of which I'd considered.)

Peaceful enough here when I return early the next morning, dew-wet but warming fast with the sun, meadow katydids already giving their stuttering, buzzy calls. I settle in, admiring the canvas of the meadow—the grasses and forbs, greens and ochres, splashes of color and muted pastels of late summer; the clumps of shrubs, the layers of taller seedlings and saplings around the margins, the textured blending of grassland and forest.

It's such a tranquil and visually appealing spot that for quite a while, as I sit and jot random notes, it blocks a simple fact that should always be at the forefront of a naturalist's mind when in such an ecosystem—the belated recognition that this meadow isn't a peaceful tapestry but a battleground, a tug-of-war between grass and tree, herbaceous and woody.

Here are the troops. On the side of the grassland are, of course, the grasses and sedges, but there are surprisingly few of them; it's mostly forbs in this meadow, goldenrod of various flavors, yarrow and clover, cinquefoil and strawberry, henbit and Queen Anne's lace, butterfly weed and three species (that I can distinguish) of thistle, dogbane and bush clover, black-eyed Susans and great blue lobelia.

The forest stands close-hemmed and overshadowing, for the opening is small, at best fifty yards long and maybe fifteen wide. The highest rim is composed of mature pitch pine and white pine, a few droopy Norway spruces, one big red pine, and some walnuts; the next and lower tier is made up of black locust trees and dogwoods, some young ashes and oaks, and some youngsters of the canopy species.

But the shock troops, trying to win back the meadow for the woodies, are autumn olives, chest-high and scattered by the dozens. They are fast-forwarding the inevitability of the battle, but the slower fighters are there, too—seedlings of white pines like little green bottlebrushes, scragglier pitch pines, sprouts of dogwood, knee-high walnuts and ashes.

The shrubs and young trees are crowding the bluebird boxes that stand in pairs, conjoined at the back, barely rising above the tide of vegetation. Another year or two, and the olives will have won, at least as meadows are measured in bluebirds—though I suspect that whoever watches over these fields will soon bring in the brush hog and raze the upstart woodies, resetting the clock in the meadow's favor.

A permanent meadow is a human conceit. Instead of allowing it to move across the landscape at the whim of fire and wind, or disappear altogether, we tie the meadow in place, as we also tie it down in time, freezing it midway through the march of succession. Our ecological tunnel vision and short attention span lead us to repeatedly try to chain ephemera to one place, be they meadows or barrier islands, always exercising our too-human desire for control and predictability.

How would this meadow be different if, instead of a mechanical brush hog chewing up the dried goldenrod and shredding the woody plants, it were maintained by fire? We have belatedly come to the realization that fire was an essential component not just of southern and western forests but also of Appalachian systems; where else did the golden-winged warbler find its nesting jungle of low brush in the old days, the chat and the yellowthroat? Where did the heath hen nest, except in the blueberry scrubs of the Poconos and the coastal plain? Big fires that killed the canopy, low fires that cleaned up the undergrowth, ridgeline fires that maintained pitch pine and scrub oak barrens. Fires from lightning, fires from Indians, but fire reshaping the land.

I'm out of my depth here, but I must make a note to ask friends of mine who wield prescribed fire for a living—exactly how do flames tip the balance in the tension between forest and field, and especially within the plant community of the meadow itself? I know that burning is especially beneficial to little bluestem, for example, which is clumped here and there in this meadow, and that while it is death to many woodies, others, like huckleberry and sweet fern, that spread by root clones can thrive with annual fires.

Of course, the choice to use a supposedly more natural system like fire to maintain a meadow is another human conceit, because a meadow is always straining toward becoming a forest. What if we let the normal course of succession unfold all the way? But that's no less a decision than brush hogging or burning, no more natural an outcome than actively managing for bluestem and bluebirds. We can't take ourselves out of the equation.

And take a look at that list of characters on the meadow's side— from a natives-versus-aliens perspective, the meadow may be the worse end of the bargain. Yarrow, autumn olive, Queen Anne's lace, henbit, chicory, birdsfoot trefoil—the meadow is overrun with exotics, and as I move my gaze from the field as a whole to the small scale of the patch surrounding my feet, the trend holds. Looking down, I see plants I'd overlooked among the wider view: dandelion, English plantain, common plantain, crabgrass, field hawkweed. Despite the mobs of fritillaries and monarchs dancing on the *Rudbeckia* blossoms, this is Eurasian ground.

Yet how flawlessly native is that forest? I stroll over to the woods at the east end of the meadow, step twenty-five paces into the trees, and look around with a critical glance. I'd already noticed, with a sour eye, the Norway spruces along the meadow's edge, but the rest of the trees are fine—pitch pine and ash, mostly, some red maple and black locust. (That last species is a native by default, since it moved itself out of the Southeast a century ago and is as much a newcomer to these hills as the spruces.) An understory of flowering dogwood and striped maple, dense thickets of white pines that, from counting their annual whorls of branches, appear to be ten to seventeen years old.

But look lower. Japanese stiltgrass grows wherever the sunlight slants through, cheek by jowl with the hay-scented ferns; there are burdock, dandelions, scruffy autumn olives, barberry, and Norway spruce seedlings among the teaberries, partridgeberries, and wild sarsaparilla. The balance is more firmly in favor of the natives within the woods, but the invaders are everywhere. The tug-of-war isn't just between competing ecosystems but between competing hemispheres, competing regimes, competing epochs in the history of the land—and the mongrel present is winning.

Plotlines, Transitions, and Ecotones

IAN MARSHALL (2007)

Monday, January 22

The height of land on the Bluebird Trail—a bit after the mowed meadow and past the big pine to the left of the trail. A faint sleety drizzle affects the writeability of this page of my notebook—one of the hazards of taking field notes. Crows caw steadily in the woods behind me—is there an intruder in their midst?

And now some jays chime in—if their rasp can be compared to the sound of bells.

This is the spot where, on the day I showed Scott Weidensaul the ecoreflection sites, we encountered the shirtless man catching insects, and I was so impressed that both Scott and the flycatcher could identify them all—robber fly and so on. I often tell my students that knowing the names of things is the first step in becoming better acquainted with them, just as it is with the people we meet; if you don't know their names, well, it's hard to know them much at all. Not knowing the name of something in nature means you don't have a label under which you can organize your observations of that thing. All that said, I am aware that I'm not very well acquainted with much of this world I profess to love, starting with the flies.

There's a bluebird box about thirty feet in front of me. And of course that's why these small meadows along the Bluebird Trail are kept open by mowing—to create the parklike habitat that bluebirds like.

I can hear, to the southwest, occasional cars on the road. There's an unknown bird behind me repeating a raspy call, like a buzzer whose batteries are running low.

The openness here is temporary, most likely. I suspect that without mowing, these meadows would be made impenetrable by brambles in a year or two, and they would grow into young forest within a decade. About six feet in front of me stands—kneels? no, sits—a foot-high shoot aspiring to be a pine. I get up and count the needles—five—so white pine.

About half an inch of snow dusts the ground—incredibly, that's the most we've had in one shot all winter. Can you spell global warming, Mr. President? The word was in this past week that measurements showed 2006 to be the warmest year on record, like just about every other year of the past decade, as each year breaks the previous year's record. I was hoping to skate on the lake today, but it'll need another week or so—if it stays cold enough, which is a big if.

first snow
    chickadees and crows
        chat about the weather

I'm teaching plot in a class this week and so I have the standard shape of plotline in my mind—the shape of a mountain, with the foothills of exposition, the rising action of the western slope, the summit of climax, the sheer drop-off of denouement. Is it coincidence that I've paused here at the high point of the trail to sit and think and write? Am I hoping for some sort of climactic action, something to give the narrative of my walk a defining moment of epiphany?

That purpose eludes me today, as I sit and think and take notes. But there is this: as I hunch over to write, trying to protect my notebook from this light sleet, the back of my neck is exposed and I can feel the sleet there, so faint the skin doesn't even feel wet. It's not much of an epiphany, but it reminds me that I am out here in the world, among the elements, touched by the not-me.

Oh, well: onward and downward. I didn't find what I'm looking for up here today, so I'll come back another time.

when the crows' caws settle
    the snow's silence
        deepens

Same day: Back at the Environmental Center, warming by the wood stove, I'm thinking more about my search for some sort of climax up on the Bluebird Trail. The arrival at a recognizable high point may be why I love hiking up mountains so much. There is the satisfaction of reaching the clearly marked goal, and a summit usually provides a view, the elevated prospect from which you can gauge where you're going and where you've been. And of course there is the tidy way in which ascent of a mountain imitates the shape of a narrative plotline—it arrives somewhere and returns. But hiking in Pennsylvania, one becomes accustomed to high points that are pretty much indistinguishable from the long line of whatever ridge you happen to be traversing. John Tallmadge in *Meeting the Tree of Life* has written about the same sort of thing in an essay about canoeing on lakes—you never achieve that high point that provides perspective or a climax to the story. And that point is what I was looking for and not finding on the Bluebird Trail.

It occurs to me that haiku offers us (by which I mean me) a different way of experiencing the natural world—that is, if we insist on trying to render that experience in some literary fashion. Forget about story, narrative, plot, climax, resolution. What haiku does is bring images together in some sort of fruitful juxtaposition, lets them resonate with and against one another, and deliberately avoids resolution, preferring open-endedness, irresolution, suggestiveness.

Doug Wentzel, naturalist and program director here at Shaver's Creek, walking by and pausing to chat as I type, thinks the raspy iterated call I heard might be a titmouse.

Haiku, it occurs to me now, is an art of the ecotone, the line where two ecosystems meet—like where I sat along the Bluebird Trail, looking out at the meadow with the forest at my back, while winter had yet to fully assert itself at the cusp of this new year. In haiku, those merging "ecosystems" could be images, or they could be language styles. Koji Kawamoto has written of the "base" and "superposed" sections of haiku. The base is the main image, conveyed in concrete (sense-appealing) diction, and the superposed section is the part of the haiku that suggests meaning or context, often through a seasonal reference. He also speaks of the two different language styles of haiku—"zoku," which is the simple, unornamented, concrete, often vernacular language of the base; and "ga," the more generalized language that owes something to the more formal poetic tradition of *renga*, from which haiku emerged.[1] (A *renga* is a group poem, usually composed by two to four poets, which begins with a three-line "hokku," to which a two-line stanza is added by the next poet, then a three-liner, and so on, with the poets taking turns. That opening stanza sets the scene, and so creating a good hokku became an art unto itself, and that's what became the art of haiku.)

In haiku, then, you have a contained area where two images and two language styles meet. It is built on the aesthetics of the ecotone. (So too is the hybrid prose-plus-haiku form of *haibun*, which I am engaging in here.) And since haiku continually plays with the idea of constancy amid change—well, that great theme also makes the Bluebird Trail seem apt territory for haiku. Individual bluebirds come and go, the seasons come and go, this meadow too will come and go—but the revolving cycle of the seasons, the calls of birds known and unknown, the feel of sleet on the back of the neck—these go on and on.

Monday, February 12

I saw a muskrat by the Troll Bridge on my way up here. He must have slipped into the water at the one patch of the creek not yet frozen over, or else he had a lair in the streambank very near where I saw him.

High twenties today—warmest it's been in a couple of weeks. Clearly, winter arrived since I was up here last month. I actually did not get out and walk last week because it was too cold, even for me—hovering around zero.

Despite the cold, the snow melted (or evaporated?) off the south-facing slope of the big meadow on the way up here.

Following up on some of my thoughts from a month ago, thinking still about how quickly the open meadows of the Bluebird Trail would be taken over by forest if they weren't mowed—I've got transitions on my mind. Of course, transitions are rarely marked by precise dividing lines, not even from season to season. Global warming has been in the news the past week or two, with the third IPCC report recently appearing and policymakers finally admitting that there just might be something to this global warming thing. Some states have begun taking the lead in energy research as the federal government continues to waffle about taking any action and to deny that there's a problem. Amid all this, my thought is that the cold snap the past couple of weeks is not so much fodder for the naysayers, skeptics, and deniers as it is evidence that the slide into global climate change, too, will not be marked by any emphatic dividing line, like the absence of winter one year. It'll be like this—arriving later each year, leaving earlier, so people may barely notice the difference from one year to the next. "This is the way the world ends," said T. S. Eliot in "The Hollow Men," "Not with a bang but a whimper."[2]

But everything is eternally in transition—consider the current ecological thinking that challenges the idea of forest succession leading to a climax forest where an ecosystem supposedly stays stable, unchanging. That stable state is a fiction, says the current science, since change is the one constant—a tree falls here and lets in light on the forest floor, a windstorm hits, or flood, or lightning, or fire, and then a human or a deer unwittingly carries—on lug sole or hoof, wool sock or fetlock—the seed of an exotic species into a piece of suddenly cleared sunlit space, and look, something new grows there. The point is that things are always in transition.

We often think of the "good old days" on this continent predating the arrival of Europeans, and we hear stories of the incredible abundance of nature in pre-Columbian America. But Charles C. Mann in his book *1491* suggests that we should not mistake the first recorded glimpses of the American continent as accounts of any sort of climax state. The abundant flocks of passenger pigeons and herds of bison—darkening eastern skies and the Great Plains, respectively—were the result of ecosystems in flux and already out of balance. What had changed, mainly, was the disruption of their main predators, *Homo sapiens*, in the form of Native American populations decimated by disease—disease whose spread accompanied the advance of white settlers.

It strikes me that accepting the concept of eternal flux would help us live our lives with less angst. Our children will grow up, the nature of our relationships will change, the circumstances of our jobs will be altered. And yet at the same time, we seek to maintain a system—an ecosystem, a way of life—by artificially fending off change. Essentially, we're managing an ecosystem—a way of life— like the Indians did pre-1492. Or like the good people of Shaver's Creek are doing here by trying to preserve bluebird habitat. When the changes going on around us are not good ones—like the loss of habitat for bluebirds or tree-hugging humans—it may be wise for us to resist change. The challenge is to balance the forces of constancy and change.

It's actually pretty comfortable sitting here in a bare patch under a white pine, snow all around, my gloves off—not too cold at all.

It occurs to me now that the hole in the stream ice where the muskrat disappeared earlier on my walk—that was also managed habitat. Why had that one turn in the stream not frozen over? Because the muskrat is keeping it open—so he can escape from the approaching clomp of critters larger than he is. I guess that would be me.

Monday, March 5

The sap is rising in the maples as we begin to have some warmer days after below-freezing nights. The maple harvest festival, one of the highlights of the year here at Shaver's Creek, is a couple of weeks away.

> snow falling lightly
>   woodpecker on a maple
>   tap-tap-taps

NOTES

1. See Koji Kawamoto, *The Poetics of Japanese Verse: Poetics, Structure, Meter*, translated by Stephen Collington, Kevin Collins, and Gustav Heldt (Tokyo: University of Tokyo Press, 2000), 125–28, 66–67.

2. T. S. Eliot, "The Hollow Men," https://allpoetry.com/The-Hollow-Men.

Caught in the Web

JOHN LANE (2016)

I'm sitting here taking notes in the Bluebird Meadow. Well, that's not completely accurate. It's midday, and I'm tucked down the trail a little to get out of the August sun. Insects buzz around. I've read "this place has stories to tell" on the plaque and I've read Scott Weidensaul's excerpt from 2006, ten years ago now. Scott calls the meadow not "a peaceful tapestry" but "a battleground, a tug-of-war" between clearing and forest. I see that clearly, so I ponder the opening for a moment and wonder what metaphors I might leave behind here as well—I'm interested in story, but it's only one of my modes of processing experience and place. As a poet, I'm also very interested in the lyric response:

> This poem includes the repetitions
> of squirrel sighs, and the buzz of the short-
> lived and ready to sleep—the grass
> trail right here at the hump of the hill.
>
> This poem has already lost the names
> of the settlers, and the heat from the nearby
> Monroe furnace cooled down centuries ago—
>
> If there is a story in this poem
> it is a very spiny one,
> like the carapace of a spider in the trail
> whose web has three slender anchors.
> If I am Shaver's Creek's storyteller then
> I am caught in more than one web.

A New Sound

KATIE FALLON (2016)

Adorable signs marked the Bluebird Trail: wooden squares with a raised wooden bluebird in the center. My constant companions on this rainy morning included wood thrushes, ovenbirds, red-eyed vireos, and an occasional scarlet tanager. Rain pooled in the center of may-apple leaves, and it occurred to me that perhaps this was the reason for their broad leaves—to funnel rainwater down the stems, to where their milky-white flowers bloom. About half of the mayapple leaves sheltered flowers, a single flower per plant. They grew together at the bases of trees, among ferns. Some of the ferns were still unfiddling, still unfurling—it had been a cool, rainy spring. Deer tracks sank deep into the trail's mud. I stepped around and over them. Next to me, a vine winding down a gnarled tree trunk moved. Not a vine: a black snake, thick and slow. The snake slipped down the trunk, flicking its tongue. We made eye contact, but I don't think it saw me; its eyes were milky. Soon the snake would shed that old itchy skin, growing larger still.

I seemed to be the only human on the trail this morning, but I was far from alone: the birds, the snakes, the unseen deer, black bears, certainly small rodents, insects and spiders, of course, and the spreading, blooming, leafing-in diversity of plant life. The trail began to climb, then switched back, and then switched back again, between thick tree trunks, moss, more mayapple. A wood thrush sang, close. I heard the gentle trill at the end of his song, and another counter-sang from further uphill. I stopped and placed my palm on a thick sugar maple trunk, leaned into the rough bark, and inhaled deeply. I heard the raindrops hitting the leaves above me and suddenly I was grinning. This magic place. These wet woods, ferns, ethereal birdsong. This is what holds me in Appalachia.

I began walking the narrow, muddy trail again, thinking about my relative aloneness. Although the space around me was absent of physical humans, other people were here with me in the forest. In his groundbreaking book *The End of Nature*, Bill McKibben uses the metaphor of a chainsaw to illustrate this phenomenon. While hiking alone in the woods, he sees "nothing to remind [him] of human society. . . . But once in a while someone will be cutting wood farther down the valley, and the snarl of a chain saw will fill the woods. It is harder on those days to get caught up in the timeless meaning of the forest, for man is nearby." Because humans have altered the earth's climate, McKibben claims, "the noise of that chain saw will always be in the woods. . . . Even in the most remote wilderness . . . the sound of that saw will be clear, and a walk in the woods will be changed—tainted—by its whine." He argues that the idea of nature as something spiritual, something beyond human, has come to an end because we have changed the "most basic forces around us"— atmosphere, temperature, weather. "We go to the woods in part to escape," McKibben writes, "but now there is nothing except us and so there is no escaping other people."[1]

Although the way humans have changed the climate seems wholly negative and the damage almost insurmountable, McKibben finds other signs of humans "almost comforting, reminders of the way that nature has endured and outlived and with dignity reclaimed so many schemes and disruptions of man." On his walk, McKibben discovers old stone chimneys, plastic chairs set along a creek for fishing, and evidence that sections of the forest were once farms. He calls these ruins "humbling sights, reminders of the negotiations with nature that have established the world as we know it."

When I assign excerpts from *The End of Nature* to my Writing Appalachian Ecology students at West Virginia University, almost universally they find McKibben's outlook bleak. I understand why. I agree that the text isn't overtly hopeful in regard to climate change, but I think it's important for us to reflect on the ways in which we affect and alter our environment in general—not only with respect to the climate but also in how we use the land, construct our homes, produce our food, and affect the other animals with which we share ecosystems. It can help us understand how we got here, and allow us to realize the part we play in an ongoing, unfolding story. Here at Shaver's Creek and Stone Valley, the land-use history is sometimes on display for us—at Twin Bridges, for example, and the Rudy Sawmill. There, families forged a living and left their marks on the land. We can still see them more than a hundred years later. McKibben sees trees dying from acid rain and it reminds him that "presidents of the Midwest utilities who kept explaining why they had to burn coal," and the "congressmen who couldn't bring themselves to do anything about it," were walking with him in the forest, too. Here, on this damp morning, pulling myself up switchbacks beneath the wood thrush, I walked with the four Rudy brothers, who turned felled trees into posts, and with the civil engineers who raised the dam that made Lake Perez, and with Rebecca Erb and her eight children near Twin Bridges.

I kept walking the crowded, lonesome trail, wondering if the red-eyed vireos that sang from the dripping trees today were the grandchildren (with one hundred greats) of red-eyed vireos that sang above the Shawnee, above the Susquehannock. Ghosts seemed to float in the mist around me, but before long the air sweetened, and I emerged into a meadow lined with autumn olives and young pines. Gray clouds hung in the sky above thin trees, still leafing out, and clumps of dense shrubs that were taller than I was. In grassy clearings between pockets of brush, nest boxes stood on posts. An interpretive sign explained that the boxes were erected in 2002 as part of an Eagle Scout project to aid the faltering eastern bluebird population. I heard one of this meadow's namesakes singing from a small tree above the shrubs. The early successional habitat in this area was popular with several bird species in addition to bluebirds; common yellowthroats and eastern towhees sang—*wichity witchity witchity* and *drink your tea!*—and—there, that buzz again—golden-winged warbler?

I began stalking the buzzing bird, following the edge of the meadow, moving slowly. The bird sang unseen among the autumn olive shrubs, and it was difficult to tell whether branches trembled beneath a bird or a drop of falling rain. I passed a jumble of cut stones, and I realized that this was what remained of an old foundation. Someone's home had been here. Did they farm this meadow? Or had this plot still been forest then? I wondered what made them build a home here, what they loved about this land. I knew what McKibben meant about these being "humbling sights"—reminders of someone who'd been here and would always be here, who had "negotiated" with nature, altered the landscape and left it altered. Beautifully altered, I thought; I liked the way the stone slabs had slid off one another but still retained the rough shape of a home, still gave enough clues to make me wonder about who had been here before. They walked with me now, too.

I heard the buzzing warbler again and set off, this time leaving the trail and wandering into higher grass. The rain-drenched blades soaked my pant legs, but I trudged on, doing my best to be quiet. *Bzz—bzz—*

bzz! It seemed as if the bird taunted me. I hadn't brought my binoculars because of the rain, but I continued to creep carefully after the bird, and I recorded its song on my phone. (Later, Doug and Jon at Shaver's Creek decided that it could have been a golden-winged warbler, a blue-winged warbler, or a hybrid. But without a visual we couldn't say for sure.)

Finally, the bird stopped buzzing, and I decided to return to the path. I turned in a slow circle and scanned the trees for the small wooden squares that marked the Bluebird Trail. I didn't see any, so I tried to follow my footsteps back through the wet grass. I stumbled upon another set of old stone foundations, and from somewhere in the distance, a dog barked. I was reminded again of Bill McKibben's chainsaw. The rain picked up, and I tightened my hood over my hat. It felt cleansing, renewing, and natural. But, McKibben asks, "how can there be a mystique of the rain now that every drop . . . bears the permanent stamp of man? Having lost its separateness, its loses its special power." I understand his point, and I feel that spiritual loss too. But perhaps, ultimately, it's better for the forest if we understand how intimately linked our actions are to its health—to these trees, this meadow. We've altered the soil here, the vegetation. We've trimmed things to encourage other things to thrive. We've put up boxes to mimic tree cavities. We blazed a trail, designed a sign, encouraged reflection. Perhaps with the knowledge of how our lives can alter the very forces of "nature," we will learn to be better residents, better caretakers—in both permanent and temporary ways. Perhaps we will still hear McKibben's chainsaw wherever we go, but maybe we'll also hear a wood thrush, and a golden-winged warbler, and raindrops on sugar maple leaves. Maybe this music can harmonize to produce a new sound—one we couldn't have imagined when we worked here a hundred years ago, perhaps one we haven't fully figured out yet in the present—but a song that those who come after us will sing with confidence because they will have learned the notes.

I glanced up at the gathering storm clouds and noticed a wooden bluebird sign on a tree—there, my trail. I joined everyone else and walked into the forest alone.

NOTE

1. Bill McKibben, *The End of Nature* (New York: Random House, 1999), 40, 76–77. The quotations from McKibben that follow are on pp. 75–76, 77, and 179.

Lake Perez

"If there is magic on this planet," wrote Loren Eiseley, "it is contained in water."[1] And where is water contained? In sea—cloud—glacier—river—lake—fog. For water is fluid stuff, taking the shape of many containers. The particular patch of water we call Lake Perez is particularly magical stuff, it seems, having pulled off in the past decade a remarkable disappearing act—when it was emptied while the dam was being repaired—then reappearing seven years later. We think of a lake as a relatively permanent feature of a landscape, but just look at the variety of forms Lake Perez has taken as the writers collected here have glided on and paddled it, pondered it and wandered through it—it's been a frozen surface to skate upon, a dry lakebed become a marsh, an invisible presence shrouded in fog, and a liquid surface that can hold a canoe on top while yielding almost unimaginably deep histories below the surface. And yet through it all it has yielded a fine reflective surface.

It's the most prominent feature in the Stone Valley Landscape, of course. The cabins at the recreation area look out on it, a short trail from the Shaver's Creek Environmental Center loops down to it, the Lake Trail circumambulates it. To get to the lake from the Bluebird Meadow, you finish the Bluebird Meadow loop and link back up with the Lake Trail, then cut across a meadow to the Troll Bridge over a thin feeder stream that runs into the lake. From the Troll Bridge you can head left and uphill to return to the Environmental Center, or go right and out to the Sunset Pavilion, perched picturesquely above the lake and commanding a view of the cabins at Stone Valley to the east, the dam at the far southern end, and the inlet here at the northwestern corner, where tundra swans sometimes drop in during the northern migration in the spring.

NOTE

1. Loren Eiseley, "The Flow of the River," in *The Immense Journey: An Imaginative Naturalist Explores the* *Mysteries of Man and Nature* (New York: Vintage Books, 1959), 15.

The Lake on Ice

IAN MARSHALL (2007)

Monday, January 29

Exhilaration! I started my walk today, intending to head up the Bluebird Trail, but saw that the ice now extends under the Troll Bridge that goes over the little stream that runs into Lake Perez south of the Environmental Center. I walked over to the dock near the end of the peninsula and then out onto solid ice. Then back to the car for skates and a hockey stick, which I'd happened to leave in the car after playing at the rink in Altoona a few days ago.

Cold sank through to the bone as I laced up the skates and then headed into the wind. I moved clockwise around the lake, exploring coves and bays along the way, touching with my stick (no puck with me) the shore at the dam end and by the cove where the civil engineering students race their concrete canoes in the spring, and the dock by the Civil Engineering Lodge. It took just fifteen minutes to go around, including pauses to look at my tracks in the inch of snow that covers much of the lake. Interesting to see how one stride commences before the other is completed, so there is a short stretch where you have two strides together, but moving away from each other. Left skate, right skate, like close quote, open quote, or closing and opening parentheses, over and over. Single quotes, of course, for quotes within quotes.

The smoothest ice seemed to be the patches where there was just a dusting of snow. Other spots had sludgy snow about an inch deep, hard to glide through, and there were some upraised ridges, where snow had drifted, perhaps, and melted down atop the ice, then refrozen, or perhaps where ripples had kept the ice from freezing smoothly. These could be skated through, but more often I hopped over them. Fifteen minutes around (it takes forty-five to walk around), then I went back to the civil engineering cove and re-skated the smoothest patches.

I chatted with an ice fisherman for a few minutes. He showed me how he measured the line and set the contraption with the flag to signal when there is a fish on the line. Catching trout and perch, he said. He used minnows for bait, dangling them about six inches off the bottom.

When I had first thought about the pond itself as a site for eco-logical reflection, I was thinking of something much quieter and more subdued than my gliding gallivant of the past hour. After all, I thought, what better spot for "reflection" than the surface of a lake—a mirror that can never crack, as Thoreau said of Walden, whose sur-face, for all its ripples, never shows a wrinkle. Shows the difficulty I have trying to see myself clearly—I go to the reflecting surface only when it has turned opaque with ice and is dusted with snow. Maybe that explains the strange colors I've been seeing in my beard lately. Must be snow on the mirror at home as well.

I wrote an article once about Thoreau's comments on skating, mostly from his journals but some from *Walden* and his essay "A Winter Walk." Thoreau was apparently a very good skater, and he was avid about it, skating up to thirty miles a day on the Concord River. Thoreau's fellow citizens of Concord, Nathaniel Hawthorne and Ralph Waldo Emerson, also skated. Nathaniel's wife, Sophia, describes Hawthorne skating "like a self-impelled Greek statue, stately and grave." She describes Emerson as being "too weary to hold himself erect, pitching headforemost"—which seems such an appropriate way for Emerson to fall; he always seemed to me so much more a poet of the mind than of the body. What Emerson described in theory about human relations with the natural world, Thoreau tried to put into practice in the way he lived. Thoreau apparently was the best skater of those famous Concord writers, performing, according to Sophia, "dithyrambic dances and Bacchic leaps on the ice."[1]

I won't claim for my own skating such balletic exuberance as Thoreau was capable of, but my hour or so of skating on Lake Perez leads me to realize that one of the reasons we go to woods and ponds is to renew our acquaintance with our physical selves. We escape to nature, surely, for spiritual reasons (to get in touch with the world or with the self, or to experience some sort of psychic rejuvenation) and for intellectual reasons (to learn about the world around us, to satisfy our curiosity about the places on maps that are not checkerboarded and gridded by roads). But part of the delight comes from experienc-ing life in a physical way, walking, hiking, climbing, paddling, skiing, skating. Out in the woods, we have to rely on our bodies and not our machines to get around. And aside from using our muscles, it also feels good to exercise our senses so fully, to use our vision both up close in examining the grain in the ice and far away in perusing the raised horizon of the surrounding hills. Same thing with our hearing, with sounds both near and far—the crunch and rumble of a skate blade over the ice and a birdcall, faint, deep in the woods, and the breeze along the shore providing soothing white pine noise. Scientists and literary critics alike are on guard against projecting human emotions onto other creatures, careful not to claim that their emotional responses or thought processes are akin to ours. What the biologist calls anthropomorphism the literary critic calls the pathetic fallacy. But it's not much of a stretch at all to imagine that other mammals, at least, must perceive and experience the world in a very similar way to us in terms of their physical relationship to it. I mean, we've all got legs and eyes and ears. It is at the level of physical being that we may feel ourselves most connected to other living things.

And, my goodness, it sure feels good to walk, or to skate, to be in the world as a physical being, to look at the sheer variety of what there is to see from the lake—the stretch of the horizon, the curves of my skate strides carved into black ice. And to hear my skates rumble and sizzle across hard ice, and to pause and hear apparent silence at first, and then a snatch or two of what the trees are saying to the breeze. And then to skate again, feel wind against my face and then to realize that it's not the air moving, it's me. The psychologist Mihaly Csikszentmihalyi (pronounced CHICK-sent-me-HIGH-ee) (which is fun to say), in a book called *Flow: The Psychology of Optimal Experience*, speaks of the concept of "flow," as in being "caught in the flow." He is referring of course to those moments of total absorption in experience, such that you cease to be aware of the self as self, which seems to me to be what haiku poets strive for but is also something athletes are very familiar with. Once they are caught up in the rhythm of a game, athletes say they react without thinking. Csikszentmihalyi says the state of flow is most likely to occur amid challenging activities that require skill to accomplish, such that we are focused on and absorbed in the task at hand. When we succeed at those challenging activities because our skills have become second nature to us, that's when we experience that sense of a self that is inseparable from the world around us, and that's when we get so wrapped up in the activity that we can lose all sense of time and can step outside the boundaries of time. In the final chapter of *Walden*, Thoreau describes the artist of Kouroo striving to carve the perfect walking staff, taking all the time he needs to seek the best possible wood, and focusing intently on his carving—and while he was so absorbed in his task, whole civilizations rose and fell around him.

I suppose if I stepped or skated out of time out there on Lake Perez, it didn't last long. My watch showed that less than an hour had passed before I was back on the dock unlacing my skates. But my fingers were no longer as cold as they had been when I was putting the skates on. I was warm throughout. My blood flowed, and my heart beat a little quicker, and I knew what it meant to be alive.

> looking back on skate tracks
>   the figure I cut
>   open quote, close quote

NOTE

1. Ian Marshall, "Winter Tracings and Transcendental Leaps: Henry Thoreau's Skating," *Papers on Language and Literature* 29, no. 4 (1993): 459–60.

Wet Earth

TODD DAVIS (2008)

The lake is half drained, and where water slid
away fast, cracks have appeared, as has the detritus

of our living. Geese seek out the few places fish
still swim, and killdeer set up home near the cinder-

blocks and tires that served as nests of another kind.
Tree stumps line the lakebed, solid despite years

submerged. I imagine this grove before any ax
cleared it, before the stream at the far side

was dammed and this depression in the earth
accepted the weight of water. A blue jay

in an ash tree sneers at our efforts, and the smell
of wet earth drying is everywhere.

Spring Melt

TODD DAVIS (2008)

Water remakes
what was made
before and reforms
itself in the bed
of its own making.
Its surface reflects
cherry blossoms,
moon's ivory
cut and placed
at petal's edge.
See the floating bridge:
how it always moves,
how we dip our fingers
in this very spot
yet touch the sea.

Lake Perez: Reflections

JULIANNE LUTZ WARREN (OCTOBER 2015)

Dust from massive exploded stars—vast clouds of atoms of every sort—by gravity, collected into earth—from its hot core to soil- and water-covered bedrock to frozen poles, with the whole of life, reaching to the skies, energized with sunlight—including today's maple and hemlock trees, club mosses, shiny red autumn meadowhawks, blue-headed vireos, Carolina wrens, pied-billed grebes, and people, like me, who have enjoyed the surroundings of Lake Perez.

From deep time and space above and below the gleaming water that floated my canoe was a history of changes and consequences. On this beaming afternoon, I let my paddles rest, soothed by the splish of their drips rippling the surface of the lake. The wind was calm. I drifted.

Seven years ago, this half-century-old, seventy-two-acre human-made lake was drained for dam renovation. The sneaky flow of Shaver's Creek had been seeping underneath the barrier. A year ago, the repair work done, the lake was allowed to refill and was stocked with a thousand bass, with more to come. Thereafter, presumably, water's, if not fishes', only way out (evaporation and hooks aside) is over the spillway.

Through those dried-up years, a brushy meadow had rooted into soil no doubt enriched by lacustrine detritus. I picked up my paddles and, from the thirty-foot deeps, headed lazily toward Twin Bridges, that is, toward the northeast curves of the lakeshore. Here, the water was more shallow. The tops of shrubs and small trees—probably aspen, black locust, glossy buckthorn, and willow—jutted out. These youngsters must have been surprised when their ground was reflooded. Some of their branches were just high enough to scratch the belly of the boat as I passed over.

I tried to see down to the lake bottom, but it was still deep enough to be dark. This was just the sort of thing to get my imagination wandering. Of course, I knew this had been an ordinary meadow just a few short months ago, but what if I time-traveled? Astride the treetops I could squint into the water, discovering past worlds beneath.

My mind first swam into a relatively recent past—a centuries-old forest community, which had grown to include big oaks, maples, white pines, hemlocks, beeches, hickories, and chestnuts—with complexly interacting earlier people—Shenks Ferry, Onojutta-Haga, Susquehannocks, Iroquois, Lenni-Lenape, and Shawnee. Then, just a few human generations ago, this whole land community was appropriated by European newcomers who turned this ground into farmland. In the middle of the 1800s, these people also burned many trees into charcoal to fuel furnaces to smelt iron ore to make stoves to burn wood and coal to heat spreading towns, build railroads, mine more mines, and develop a nation. Some of the ore used was local. Here in the deeps under my floating vessel, the nineteenth-century pioneers had mined a seam.

Then I rushed back more than 400 million years ago, long before mammals and birds had distinguished themselves, when this place actually lay close to the equator. The ancient Taconic Mountains were weathering, releasing large quantities of iron atoms, which gravity pulled downhill, into rivers washing through an alluvial plain into the newly formed Appalachian Basin. Scaly fish were just developing in the rivers. As I happened to be near a stream, I followed it down into the basin's trilobite-crawling, coral-growing ocean. These briny waters were remnants of the far older, wider-spread Iapetus Sea. I swam at least another 100 million years back, surrounded by gobs of jellyfish and worms and mounds of photosynthesizing blue-green algae—already distinguished by billions of years of global atmosphere-transforming history—yet another ancient world under this lake.

I stood for a very, very long time, watching the Taconic Mountains wear down. Then I saw, just 350 million years ago, colliding landmasses grow other peaks, the Acadians, just east of today's Pennsylvania. These mountains also eroded into the old Appalachian marine basin, widening its shores with heavy deposits, which kept coming, weighting down the ground all around, over time, pressing it into stacks of black and gray shale. Climates slowly shifted over this ground. So did saltwater margins, seasons of heavy rains and drier times, sediment-bearing rivers, and swamps with lush plants, featuring tropical trees and ferns, and animals, including insects and fishes' young descendants, air-breathing amphibians. Repeatedly, swamps' fallen leaves and trunks became peat and, along with scales and fleshy bodies, were unhurriedly buried with sand and mud, compacted, and transformed into an abundance of carbon-rich coal. Here, then, another series of worlds extended through the reaches below me.

Next, I felt earth tremble with the rise of the area's biggest mountains of all—the Alleghanians. These giants were thrust two and a half miles high by another continental crash 300 million years ago. Bedrock heaved, angled up and stood on end, was folded, bent, squeezed, and fractured. Water, as it still does, went wherever it could, so it infiltrated many new-formed nooks and crannies. Meanwhile, the sea of the Appalachian Basin had receded, leaving in its wake hundreds of millions of years' worth of accumulated layers of mud mixed with the remains of marine life tamped down under eroding mountain sediments. The mud and decayed plants and animals— whose bodies stored the energy of ages of sunlight mixing with atoms—compressed and heated underground, were slowly transformed into roving varieties of fossil hydrocarbons: petroleum. Like water, oil and gas migrate, which they did through unfathomably intricate networks of pores, fissures, and cracks in the aged tiers of their hardened-mud shales and other rocks. In a few places, they seeped—whether black and gooey or light and bubbly—right out of the ground. In most cases, the stuff was held tight in reservoirs as much as several miles down, far beneath coal and iron mines, in this even older realm.

Though my exploration of other worlds was worlds away from complete, I needed to breathe. My mind popped up into the sunlight, into my boat, still skimming the branches of the past year's brushy meadow's sapling trees, mostly hidden underwater. A great blue heron flew overhead in the direction of the old Sawmill Site.

Through long geological ages, the immediate Shaver's Creek vicinity seems to have kept on the drier side of the ancient sea plain's ridges and valleys, and it was also less peaty. Just a few miles south, though, in the same county, is a borough that mid-nineteenth-century miners named "Coalmont" in the township called "Carbon." And two counties west lies the border of the state's most significant area of oil and gas.

Today, miners are drilling wells to increasing depths—in some cases now nearly two miles down, perhaps as far as the Iapetus Sea bottom. Today, miners are using deep-ground explosives to crack open the foundations of fossil-rich bedrock. Over the past decade, with this twenty-first-century earth-quaking technology called hydraulic fracturing, miners—with some but not all citizens' permission, yet with consequences to everyone—are injecting pressurized air, water, sand, mud, and rock-dissolving chemicals into partly understood yet unfathomable realms to flush out petroleum. Unknown brews of mixing molecules thus are moving uncertain distances at uncertain speeds into the vast sunken network of pores and fissures—sometimes, to be sure, burbling aboveground, into drinking glasses and crop fields, seeping into webs of lives of lakes and rivers, running into oceans. As a result of this mining procedure, natural gas—in other words, the potent greenhouse gas methane—also is leaking into the atmosphere in record quantities. All that miners can capture of the earth's long-secreted carbon-rich matter and energy appears destined for burning into an increasingly heat-trapping sky in order to turn on electricity, move cars and planes, make plastic toys and plastic guns, and fuel the growth of an industrial global economy—which, even so, for life to prosper, requires refreshing waters and a comfortable earth-blanket of air.

As I said, not all wheels can be kept turning.

I returned to the lake the next morning, the twenty-second, amid a pastel dawn—billowing with golden-pink, gray, and white clouds against a baby-blue dome. I caught the mirrored image of that sky and the black-green shoreline on the surface of the water, shadowing into the shade of my canoe. This gave the illusion of a world upside-down, with the trees rooted in the sky, crowns dangling. Now I was floating in air.

How does one learn the stories of air, old or new? Like those of the stars and the ground, they, at least in part, are written deep into earth—for example, in the chemistry of buried water; in compositions of fossilized life, including coal and petroleum; in rock formations; in bubbles trapped in ocean mud and glacial ice. Atmosphere's tales are told by gauges measuring proportions of gases in the air—with far higher concentrations of greenhouse gases now than at any time in human history, with consequences rippling—in temperatures on mountaintops and sea surfaces, marine acidity, flows of musical creeks and respiration rates of forests. The stories of air are drawn in conditions of soils and birds—in earth's whole diversity of life.

Stories of earth may also be disclosed now in terms of generations of human flourishing—for richer or poorer, in sickness or health—yesterday, today, and in centuries and longer ages to come. Time and place tell on us, revealing whether or not we attuned our commonweals with the turning wheels that mean life.

Leavings, October 23

The shining moon had thickened from talon-curved to spotted-egg-shaped over the course of my Shaver's Creek week. My car was packed. I felt myself shiver, though there was only the slightest breeze and the temperature was ten above freezing. One last time, I slid my canoe off the grassy shore and into the water. I headed out, taking care to dip my paddle silently. What is it about darkness that desires peace and quiet?

Stars glimmered overhead. Between strands of mist smoking low over the surface of the lake, pins of light appeared to originate from its depths. Suspended between earth and moon, I felt myself true—made mostly of water coursing through a temporary frame built of ancient stellar dust.

It was hard to make out the shoreline, but I guessed I might be somewhere near the lake's middle when I stopped, once more, to listen. I heard the occasional whines of trucks flying by on an outlying road joined by the voices of darkness-concealed waterfowl softly creaking around my boat. From the far shore came a mutual echoing: a barred owl called out low and rhythmically. From the hills beyond, another countered quickly, in higher-sounding tones, finishing with a wild scream.[1]

NOTE

1. I thank my good friend Dr. John H. Barnes and his co-author, W. D. Sevon, for their *Geological Story of Pennsylvania*, 3rd ed. (Harrisburg: Pennsylvania Department of Conservation and Natural Resources, 2002), so helpful to my explorations of Lake Perez.

Fog on Lake Perez

JOHN LANE (2016)

Day 1

> Fog is the last visitor of night,
> Lingering at the doorway to deeper
> Rooms than morning. There is a dark
> Curtain reflecting pines, then the window
> Closes, and the birds fly through.
> Crows are doorbells. Woodpeckers
> Mock the solidness of standing wood.
> A kingfisher knocks too with its call,
> But the lake answers no, so the bird
> Flies over the fog, which drifts in
> Only one direction—earthward,
> Trying to marry water, but the ceremony
> Isn't happening. If there is a minister
> It might be Time, or Sorrow (fog's bridesmaid)
> Or Silence. I can't tell from this distance,
> Those ideas being metaphysical and I'm
> A pragmatist. In an hour the fog will be gone—
> A function of temperature, like all magic.
> If morning has a browse line, I've reached it.

Reflection at Lunch, the Cabin
Life must seem very long to a goose. There is a raft of them near shore.
Their rhythm is slow. But then again, they don't worry about aging.
In the time it's taken me to eat four Fig Newtons, they've floated a
hundred yards north on the lake. Fifteen geese. I heard them come
in honking last night near dusk. Did they have reservations? When
is their checkout time?

Day 2

> Fog out on the lake again.

Coffee, cereal and banana
In a borrowed bowl.
My toe hurts as I kicked
A rock yesterday afternoon
Descending from the Bluebird
Meadow. Another rock
Traveled all day with me
In my pocket—Black gravel
With a white quartz
Band. Lifted from the trail
For memory, now the ballast
Of travel, this rock serves
As a paper weight as I flip
The pages of my yellow journal,
Looking for scraps of experience,
And it reminds me of what
Is beneath my feet at every step.

Last night I sat around the fire with Ian and talked Great Nature in an old fashioned way, as if the Anthropocene hadn't happened, and we agreed how much we both love the wilderness, and he admitted how much he loves this place, too, but there isn't much wilderness here, with the lake, the lodge, the trails, the highways. "All engineered," I said. "Everything is civil and engineered." But there is surprise. Yesterday Jerod walked me out back of the bathrooms at the Raptor Center to a redbud tree with a discovery on almost every leaf. He reached up and tapped a web I had not seen, and a brightly colored spider descended from a leaf lean-to on a single thread.

Geology is comforting
In an uncommon way:
We are no more than
the fur of the world.

The bones of the earth
Are always below, articulated
And dismembered by time's
Passage. There is no gospel

More certain than erosion,
Transportation, deposition.

Fog, on the other hand, is unsettling, just as it is beautiful. It drifts about, and as Sandburg said, covers all. It's solid and it's not. As we drank beer and watched the fire last night, Ian said that for seven years there was no Lake Perez when the dam went out, and "a stream meandered freely in the valley below. It's hard to believe it now."

A few minutes ago the fog was so thick the lake could be gone again. I believe all things are momentary.

Day 3

I've been thinking this morning about
The difference between reflection
And observation. Obviously there
Has to be something to be reflected—
A self, a place, a thing. With observation
There is the seeing. The idea
Of object. The lake is a thing to be
Seen, but to reflect on the lake is different.

The crows are back. Should I reflect
On them? And what would that mean?
What would I contribute? What is new
If I write here about crows this morning?
Do I have to know something new about
Crows to reflect on them? I am swaddled here
In a community of naturalists, and they
All know these things. I know some things,
But other things I don't know. If I am
An expert it is an expert in enthusiasm.
So maybe I should stick with the fog,
Something very literary? Ted Hughes
Did for crows what Carl Sandburg did
For fog. But there is a problem:
This morning there is little fog.

So I take off for the waterfront and climb
In the canoe and cast off on fogless Lake Perez.

The engineering of Dr. Perez has worked!
I recreate and reflect at the same
Time! I am intellectually ambidextrous!
Ducks preening! Painted turtles
Sunning, with bright red plasterns!
I forget about the fog. Fog is ancient
History. Fog is the Tigris and Euphrates
Of Stone Valley. Fog is no more relevant
To me this morning than Mayan petroglyphs!
But I don't forget about the crows,
As now they have moved across the lake
Where something has their attention
And they caucus relentlessly. Then as I'm
Paddling back I see a happy man in a blue
Shirt with his little daughter in his lap.
They are fishing. He has appeared since
I paddled out. He is sitting on a little point
Among the cabled canoes of the university's
Recreation program. I am paddling and reflecting,
And they are fishing and fishing and fishing.
She is laughing. And I am paddling past.
And I wave, and the man in the blue shirt
Waves back. I get out my journal and write.
We reflecting writers are like Mayan priests
Watching the night sky for generations.
What could that mean? The crows cackle
And chortle in the distance, their commentary
On my reflection is complete. But what could
It mean? I think it means that somebody has
To do this, reflect on what is and what could
Be and what connects the two—like a comet
Careening toward our place, and passing
Close by, the mysteries are out there.
We don't know close to everything. That's
Why we reflect. To find out how much space
There is, say, between the line and the fish
And the hook. That's my story, and I'm
Sticking with it, in spite of the noisy crows.

The Lake Trail

TRAILHEAD NOTE

Take away the detours to the Sawmill Site, the Chestnut Orchard, the Dark Cliffy Spot, and the Bluebird Meadow, and we, Dear Reader, have already completed the Lake Trail loop, and then some. But if you would like to take another go-round without the detours and the pauses for reflection, feel free—at a good pace, it'll take you only about an hour.

The Lake Trail, of course, is not really a place but many places— more an ecoreflection experience, achieved through the activity of a walking meditation, rather than a particular spot where you sit and think. The rhythms of the walk, the alternating strides of left foot and right, seem to have inspired the ecoreflectors collected here to meditate on the rhythms of time, or on the attractions of solitude and silence on the one hand (or foot?) and of movement and its accompanying acoustic commotion on the other. At times, the rhythms of the past seem to mingle with the present, as the physical activity of a walk puts you in the here and now, while the contemplative activity of a walk allows memory to infiltrate the perceptions of the moment. As much as a walk puts us in connection with the earth—the point of connection, of course, being the sole—a walk seems to balance the venturing outward with some process of self-discovery, or at least self-exploration. As John Muir famously put it, "I only went out for a walk, and finally concluded to stay out till sundown, for going out, I found, was really going in."[1]

This is a circumambulation, a circuit walk, keeping the lake on the right, returning where you began. And that is the path of the mythical hero, right, outward motion and return. Maybe every walk is an act of heroism, and a return—to sanity, to ourselves, to the earth.

NOTE

1. John Muir, *John of the Mountains: The Unpublished Journals of John Muir* (1938), edited by Linnie Marsh Wolfe (Madison: University of Wisconsin Press, 1979), 439.

Clockwise Around the Lake

IAN MARSHALL (2006)

Monday, April 10

> spring shoots
>   the pines show them how
>   the green thing is done

A glorious day—sun out, maybe sixty degrees. Scallions are coming up on the west side of the lake. The green of the pines seems especially vivid in the warming sun.

Construction on the boardwalk into the swamp is complete now about forty feet in. Construction workers are eating pizza and chatting as I walk by.

En route around the lake, I think of Thoreau's description of Walden Pond as "Earth's Eye," with overhanging pines as eyelashes, the surrounding tree-covered hills as brows. There are ducks skimming over the lake today, motes in earth's eye.

And Emerson, in "Circles"—"the eye is the first circle, the horizon the next, and nature endlessly repeats this figure." (That may not be an exact quote; I'm relying on memory here.) The trunks of trees, the shores of the lake, the earth in its turning, the whirl of a galaxy—circles. And me, once a week, inscribing a circle around the lake, watching the seasons and the year turn, a bit at a time—1/52 per week, to be precise. Hmm, my next birthday is my fifty-second. Once more around and maybe I too will have seen the whole cycle. How does that Issa haiku go? Something about his fiftieth birthday, and everything from here on is gravy. (Again, that's not an exact quote—and probably not even very close.)

I saw a raccoon, I think—might have been a groundhog; I didn't get a close look—by the small stream by the Bluebird Trail. He headed for the hollowed-out base of a dead tree right in the streambed. Good hunting from there, I would think, especially for a crayfish-loving raccoon. But it must be a chilly home base with the water flowing by so near.

Monday, April 24

Another circumambulation—saw the groundhog again, again near the bridge by the Bluebird Trail—and can confirm it as a groundhog (not a raccoon).

I thought of time and metaphor, and circles and lines, on the walk around the lake today. We often perceive time as an arrow—that is, linear time that leads us to see evolution as a progression leading up to us, at least in our teleological view. Or we see our own lives as progress leading up to us, now, at this point in the story of our lives. And onward to our dying day. But of course time moves cyclically as well—as in the seasons. And I suppose we could see our whole lives as cyclical—from earth we arose, to earth we return. Think of how often cyclical movements are repeated in the natural world—earth in its daily rounds, the moon around the earth, the earth around the sun, the sun one of many on a whirling galactic wheel, the hawk I saw on my walk spiraling over the ridge.

What's that Yeats line about a "widening gyre"? His image of a center that "cannot hold" has been crucial in postmodern readings of life and literature. The center—whatever anyone happens to think holds things together—God, Truth, Progress, Democracy, Nature, Law, Reality—whatever transcendental signified you put your faith in—it cannot hold. And things fall apart.

But I'm wrong, aren't I, in calling the earth's path around the sun a circle. It's an ellipsis, the path of something with two foci, not the one center focal point of a circle. I have no idea what that means in terms of transcendental signifieds, nor am I clear about what the twin foci of my life might happen to be. Literature and Nature? Self and Significant Others? Inside and Out? Me and Not Me?

I seem to be traveling a long metaphorical way from my path around the lake today. Maybe I should be writing about skunk cabbage and joe-pye weed, emerging life along the Lake Trail, instead of going in philosophical or meditative circles. But perhaps that's what literature trains the mind to do—think metaphorically. Robert Frost points out in "Education by Poetry" that thinking in metaphor is an important and high-order intellectual skill—one that can be best cultivated through the study of poetry. But he also cautions that when we ride a metaphor, we have to know when to get off. A metaphor is a way of thinking about one thing in terms of another (i.e., Lake Trail = Life), but at some point all metaphors break down, because whatever else it might represent, a cigar is just—no, not *just* but *also*—a cigar. And the Lake Trail is the Lake Trail, a walk around the lake a walk around the lake.

Oh, I surprised a pileated woodpecker—and he me—on my walk. A clatter in the brush, a flurry of flight, a quick impression of his size, the red head. Odd that he was in the brush, though, and not tapping at bugs on the trunk of a tree.

startled on a spring walk
  groundhog, woodpecker, squirrels,
     human

Monday, May 8
Post-walk around the lake: I've got to say something about the rhythm of walking. It's conducive to poetry, certainly—see Wordsworth and his blank verse excursions. Walking is so consistently iambic—two syllables combining to make a metrical foot. The fact that we call a beat of poetry a "foot"—that alone says something about the connection.

A walk does seem to be conducive to the flow of language—or maybe it's that the flow of language is the product of the workings of mind—the jaunt or journey or meanderings of mind—that a walk inspires. But why is that? Is it the physical motion that jolts or nudges the mind into its own motion? The montage of perceptions—so many things to notice at every step—as landscape seems to slide by?

Besides the poetry, there's something very human about walking. It's what we humans do well—as opposed to the snake's slither, the tiger's pounce, the impala's dead run. I mean, I know all creatures walk, but not bipedally, and we humans can do it all day long. (When we're in shape, at least.) We can cover a remarkable amount of ground on foot in a day, seeing—and thinking—and planning—all the while.

I know it's one of the things I do well. Maybe it's not much to boast of—I walk well—but it's true. When I take students out on hikes, few can keep up with me. And yet many of them are stronger and fitter than I. I guess there's some muscle memory involved, giving some fluidity to my walk that has stayed with me from days when I was strong and fit and walking the Appalachian Trail. There must be some kind of efficiency in a practiced hiker's stride—the unconscious placing of foot on angled rock or over log or around whatever other little obstacles disrupt the flow of an inexperienced walker's pace.

I note that I usually go around the lake clockwise—and it occurs to me that a walk happens in at least three kinds of time. There's the second hand of moment-by-moment perception—when you see things like the skunk cabbage still out, or that somebody's put a board over this muddy spot in the trail, the meadowsweet flowers are done already, the deciduous trees are all in leaf now, and the conifers seem to take a step back into the general forest green. Minute by minute there are small highlights anticipated and relished whenever you pause for more than a moment: a view of the new boardwalk from that open spot up there, new canoes beached on shore, hello to a fisherman, stop at the bridge over the dam and watch the patterns in the water moving down the spillway. And hourly—another circuit of the lake completed, time to write about some of what I thought about—though most of it is gone now, or never took shape as words.

But of course a walk is implicated in other sorts of time as well—daily rhythms, the cycle of the seasons, and so on. What a walk does, I think, is remind us more of certain kinds of time—especially the moment-by-moment and seasonal cycle types of time—than we typically encounter in lives that focus mostly on daily and weekly routines.

Monday, October 17
Once more around the lake—as always, clockwise. The lake as clock face—that upon which we can read the time. Currently, at every mark around the dial, the clock says autumn. Yellow, gold, orange, red, scarlet—easy to read at this time of year.

So if the lake is clock face, what am I in my weekly walk around? The second hand? No, the whole point of the walk is to experience nature firsthand.

It's the turn of the seasons, I suppose, reminding me that my walk around the lake echoes the cyclical nature of time. Despite all the round clock faces in our daily lives (maybe because they've been replaced by digital clocks?), we tend to forget that circular figure of time. We typically measure our lives in lineal time from the beginning of a semester, or a workweek, or a business quarter, or a fiscal year, and we pause at the end to measure our progress, to see how far along some line we've moved, how much further to go to reach some goal. We grow up, we grow old, we shall wear the bottoms of our trousers rolled, and we measure out our lives in coffee spoons. (Thank you, T. S. Eliot, for the convenient phrases.)

But it's not like that, is it—life, I mean. It's all cycles—water falling, flowing down rivulet, rill, and stream to a lake, evaporating out, condensing in clouds, falling again, down to the sea in molecules. Then evaporating and condensing again, falling again on dry ground, then uproot and out-leaf of plants and transpiring out to the open air, back to the clouds, back to the earth.

Walking the boardwalk today (yes, it's been completed since the spring), I saw a turtle in Shaver's Creek, legs splayed, shell tilted down to catch the current, beaked snout poked above the surface. He'd ride the slow current for a minute, then paddle a few inches, splay and float. Debris drifted past him, but he didn't try to eat any. His shell was round, marked around the edges with orange and yellow.

autumn
    painted turtle
       drifting

Circumambulating the Lake

DAVID GESSNER (2012)

Trees leaning back graciously from the trail, exposing their roots (shocking!), making me want to nod thank you as I pass. Then on to the land of skunk cabbage. I am the great circumnavigator. I remember when I cheated on that test in college. It was a gut, our word for an easy course. Its official title was something like "The History of Maritime Exploration," but we called it "Boats." I barely went to the class, and the night before the test, I borrowed my friend Riley's notes. It was going to be an essay test, and I was good at essays, so I figured if I crammed a few facts I could weave something out of them.

Sure enough, the question was about one of the subjects Riley's notes had covered. I wrote as one inspired, telling exciting tales of maritime exploration. I think what I wrote was actually pretty good, and had it not been for one small problem might have gotten me an unearned B. But that one problem did me in. The explorer I wrote of was named Rosco Tacoma. The trouble was, there was no one by that name. I had misread Riley's crimped hand and mistranscribed it into my own notes. On and on I went about brave Rosco. But the real explorer was Vasco da Gama. I can't remember if I got a low C or a D in the class.

The point? The point is that names are important. Naming is a lot of what we do as naturalists (a word I fall far short of). It is only polite to get to know the names of your neighbors. Part of the joy of the walk on the first day here was listening to Doug, Josh, and the interns as they named the birds, plants, and insects. Sometimes you could see them pause, considering, trying on a name to see if it fit. It is a vital procedure, perhaps the most basic tool of the naturalist.

On the other hand, it can be taken too far. As if naming itself were the study of nature. As if the woods were a crossword puzzle you're trying to figure out. We miss a lot if the focus is only on names.

But names at their best are a jumping-off point. They are descriptive, seeds for what is to come, containing the spirit of the greater enterprise.

I emerge in the boathouse camp. How happy I am to be where I am, and not on this side of the "lake." Poor Scott Weidensaul, the former reflector. Mowing seems to be the obsession on this side, and there is plenty to mow. I prefer my quieter side, across the nonwater. There, last night, Ian, Bob, and company all came up for a visit and a few beers. We had a fire and Ian's son, Jacy, brought out a telescope only a tad smaller than the Hubble. My favorite sight was a star cluster, a minigalaxy, millions of stars so far away. It was the first—and only—time I'll have company at my new home.

And now it's as if I've conjured it up. The cabin comes into sight across the grassy water. My heart lifts a little. My bad leg has done okay, but I'm ready for that porch and the one remaining Slab Cabin IPA (which is where I'm sitting, drinking, and writing this.)

If sex, according to the French, is a small death, then so is that moment in a walk when you decide to turn back. There is always a little sag to it, a sense that an ending has begun. Today's sag came back at the mill site.

But this, the sighting of the cabin, is different. My step picks up. The homestretch. Literally. I'm almost done, sore leg and all. As the local inspector of snowstorms, I've done my work, made my rounds. I commend myself for it, since no one else is around. Good work, David.

I pass the boats: when was the last time canoe #12 saw action? A plastic dock still acts as if it has a job to do, floating over asters, weeds, and grass. I have been generally walking over the dam, but today I veer straight for home, disqualifying me, perhaps, from true circumambulation (I'm no Rosco Tacoma) but getting me to my beer faster.

Parts of the lake bottom send me back to last week in the Grand Canyon. It is cracked, dusty, desiccated. Cracks everywhere. But then I get to the Great Puddle, just below the dam, the lake within a lake that I (bird)watch from my dock. And I see a couple new visitors. My juvenile great blue heron is not here, nor the lazy kingfisher. But a couple of killdeer are skirting along the puddle's edge. Not too exciting, you say. But—wow! As they go into their usual fakery, their bellies flash a vivid white, their brown and black rings. . . . And then another newcomer. A green heron flies off, its yellow-orange legs dangling like landing gear.

And now, as both Homer and Steely Dan sang, "home at last." Bad leg up on a chair, good beer down the gullet. I toast myself.

(I even think I might be losing a little weight. The Thoreau Workout might be worth marketing.)

The Work of Walking

DAVID TAYLOR (2013)

I'm walking the three-mile hike around the lake,
over mowed lawn,
across the rain-slick wood walkways and bridges spanning Shaver's
    Creek, around the dam construction,
up and down the trail passing hickory, sumac, oak, pine, hemlock,
listing as I go.
What is this that must be done?
Stretching out one leg then the other,
counting shrubs and trees,
noting the silver spotted skippers by their spattered ore mark,
watching a wren and listening for its call, imitating perch and
    pitch,
letting the bumblebees whirl and hum around me as I hold a stem
    of clover,
marking a cloud shifting from one ridge to another with my hand.
It's a calling to circumambulate,
a vocation to circle the mountain there, to round the lake here,
to walk the trail over and over,
again,
again,
beginning to see your own footprints.

A Place for Exuberance

One July evening, planning my next day's hike with campers around
the Lake Trail, I set out by myself. I ignored the gathering clouds,
this being my only chance to make sure I knew the route before I
led a group of kids on it. Halfway into the hike, the rain started.
Then the thunder. When I came to power-line clearings, I ducked
and ran, feeling vulnerable in the open stretches. Though it was not
past eight o'clock, the forest had darkened and the hour felt late. The
rain came so hard that the jacket I'd worn was useless. But once I
resigned myself to being wet, I no longer felt resistant to it. The trees
were wet and I was wet, and together we were beneath the storm that
was bigger than any of us. Flashes of lightning cast brief shadows.
If I'd heeded my judgment, I would have stooped down and taken
shelter, but I relished the feeling of being buffeted. My skin prickled
as the thunder closely followed the lightning. The sky sounded like
it was tearing. I made my way home safely. At the Roost (the interns'
house), my housemates looked at me for a moment gape-mouthed.
They hadn't realized I'd been out in the storm, and there I stood,
looking happily addled in my sopping clothes.

Now, as I write, it's raining again, but only hard enough for me
to hear the drops on the maple leaves above me. A raven, very near,
is saying *rawk, rawk, rawk!* I'm sitting not on the Lake Trail proper
but on Spearmint, the trail we used this summer to skirt the dam
construction when we took kids on the Lake Trail loop. This spot,
where a long plank bridge spans a muddy section of Shaver's Creek,
is where, one Thursday, my campers completed their stream study.
The water was too cloudy to find crayfish, but they discovered water
pennies, mayflies, stoneflies, dragonfly larvae, and, to their dismay,
one large leech. Their favorite part of the stream study was afterward,
when they were challenged to make boats from found materials. One
group discovered the top half of a G.I. Joe; he rode their bark boat.
Another group made a ship for a queen, which was an acorn perched

on a tiny yacht. We all cheered on the boats, seeing which one could stay afloat longest.

Hiking on the Lake Trail with campers, we'd sing camp songs. Loudly. Sometimes the same ones over and over. As someone who likes to go quietly, I struggled with instigating such raucousness—it much diminished our chance of seeing wildlife. But when the kids sang, they forgot about how far they'd walked or had yet to walk. Or that they were hot or wet. So much of the year, kids are funneled down the halls of school, where they must stay in line and keep quiet. And so, to shout, "You can't ride in my little red wagon!" at the top of their lungs—in a place where no one is going to tell them to settle down—is a blessing.

Once, I hiked with a dear friend at Ricketts Glen, a trail northeast of here featuring stunning waterfalls. He brought his ukulele and barreled out tunes in his baritone voice as we walked along. I felt embarrassed at the time, as if we had trespassed on the ears of warblers. Today, though, when I consider the volume of thunderstorms, the songs we sing on trails don't seem such an affront to the solemnity of trees. While going quietly is a valuable way of knowing, exuberance also has its place. The woods host beauty, but they are not a museum. The rain falls in torrents, lightning cracks trunks, ravens call out, and, from time to time, a pack of seven-year-olds sing till they're hoarse. The auditory disturbance will dissipate, but the connection to nature these kids develop may last a lifetime, creating the citizens who will protect these lands.

A Little Quiet, Please

MARCIA BONTA (2015)

May 23

Even though it is a gorgeous Saturday afternoon, my husband, Bruce, and I find Shaver's Creek Environmental Center fairly quiet, although a few local families have brought their children to the manicured grounds, where the adults watch and visit while the children wade in and out of the tiny pond.

As soon as we start on the trail, though, we are alone. Serenaded by a scarlet tanager, we walk past blooming golden ragwort, long-spurred violets, and sweet cicely. Nearing the boardwalk in the wetland, we see wild geranium and golden ragwort flower amid skunk cabbage leaves.

We emerge from the forest onto the boardwalk that spans a portion of the wetland, and have our first glimpse of the lake—seventy-two acres of sparkling water on which a single Canada goose floats.

Far more wildlife seems to be concentrated in the wetland. Green frogs burp their calls. Red-winged blackbirds scold from nests hidden in the shrubs and cattails. A gray catbird unravels his long string of imitative calls and songs. Below, in the water, hundreds of tadpoles swim. A tiger swallowtail slowly flutters past on its showy yellow and black wings, in contrast to the flat-winged, speedy flight of a whitetail dragonfly.

Then we are back in the forest, where ovenbirds and red-eyed vireos sing. Once again I catalogue plants—Indian cucumber-roots, mayapples, sensitive and Christmas ferns, Solomon's seals, Canada mayflowers, and Hercules' clubs in the understory. Hemlocks overhead, the undersides of some of their flat green needles showing hemlock woolly adelgid damage, look as if they have several more years, especially if the cold winters continue. But the white oaks and even some small basswoods will probably replace them, just as oaks in Pennsylvania have replaced American chestnut trees. Although I find one small chestnut tree lurking in the understory, it is doomed to die soon from the implacable fungus.

From the forest, the Lake Trail leads us onto an expansive green blanket of grass that spreads to the lake. We have reached the old Civil Engineering Camp in Penn State's seven-thousand-acre Stone Valley Recreation Area. Eleven year-round small rental cabins, flanked by a road and numerous picnic tables, have attracted families and couples bent on enjoying a sunny afternoon near or perhaps on the water in the small rowboats, paddleboats, and canoes for rent by the half hour.

But my attention centers on the strange bird flying low over the water. Its long bill, black body, and skinny head make me think it is a double-crested cormorant, and when it lands in the water, I am certain, because its profile, both flying and floating, and its diving, are cormorant-like, and I am pleased to see a bit of wildness in a decidedly managed habitat.

We wind our way past the cabins, searching for the orange blazes marking the trail, and shortly before we leave the area, a very large man on an even larger, dust-spewing mowing machine drives past, waving. If the folks on the picnic ground hope for a peaceful afternoon, they aren't going to get it.

Continuing on toward the dam breast, I note sweet ferns, wild yam root, and mapleleaf viburnums in the forest. American goldfinches bounce overhead, and an eastern phoebe perches on the fence atop the spillway. A thin sheet of water streams over the sterile cement spillway into the diverse wetland below, where a common yellowthroat sings its *witchity* song.

We pause to read the plaque explaining the origin of Lake Perez, named for civil engineering professor Lawrence J. Perez, who taught at Penn State from 1944 until 1970. He worked during the glory years of dam building in the United States and especially in Pennsylvania, where so many free-flowing streams, large and small, were dammed to please the people who preferred lakes to streams for their recreational pleasure. Perez had helped to plan, design, and construct the dam, which was finished in 1961. After all, that was what engineers did in those days and still do—build first and ask ecological questions later. Today, as dams break down and need expensive repairs, numerous small and even larger dams have been destroyed, and streams and rivers run free again. But Lake Perez was recently resurrected after several years when it was drained for repairs.

Of course, the lake is used for a variety of Penn State University's gym classes, and recently, as we learn when we walk up the gravel road leading from the spillway, Vertical Adventures for Groups has been added so that students can perfect their climbing skills, engaging in the newest and most popular recreational pastime.

On either side of the road grows an almost impenetrable hedge of bush honeysuckle, most probably Amur honeysuckle, *Lonicera maackii*, still another invasive shrub from Asia that white-tailed deer dislike. But the forest above the shrubs is native and diverse and includes both black walnut and red spruce trees.

Still, the trail only regains its interest after we pass the last of the climbing equipment, and once again becomes a footpath strewn with flowering dogwood petals. Wild grapevines twining through the trees are in greenish-yellow flower. I also note white pines and maple trees thriving in what appears to be a recovering woodland. Silver-spotted skippers and blue azures flit along the path in front of us. The understory is dominated by a dark green carpet of Virginia creeper that is frequently penetrated by more golden ragwort.

By this time, we are across the lake from the mad mower, who is still at work, destroying the peace even at this distance. And I wonder, as I hear the scream of a motorcycle on a nearby but hidden road, whether anyone notices the noise or if most people are so inured to it that they are neither aware nor bothered by it.

I am reminded of acoustic ecologist Gordon Hempton's attempt to make the Hoh Rainforest in Olympic National Park the world's first quiet zone. Increasingly distressed by the loss of natural silence because of human-made noise even in the most remote areas of the earth, Hempton found a location deep in the Hoh where he established his one square inch of silence on Earth Day 2005 by placing a small red stone on a log three miles from the Visitor Center. He hoped that if he could protect that area from noise pollution, the rest of the park would be quiet.

In his book *One Square Inch of Silence*, subtitled *One Man's Search for Natural Silence in a Noisy World*, Hempton recounts his trip across the United States from Oregon to Washington, D.C., zigzagging from one recommended quiet place to another where, as The Sound Tracker˙, he records and measures the decibel level of mostly natural sounds, producing a sonic record of America. He also hopes to meet politicians and other government officials in Washington who might be interested in noise reduction, especially in wilderness areas.

As a young man, Hempton had been inspired by John Muir's *A Thousand-Mile Walk to the Gulf*, where Muir wrote, "There is nothing more eloquent . . . than a mountain steam," several decades before our love affair with dam building began in the early twentieth century. Hempton devoured Muir's books, writing that Muir's "listening prowess and ability to capture the varied range of nature's symphony astounded me."[1]

Following in Muir's footsteps, Hempton went to Yosemite National Park, grew a beard, and even followed a wilderness vegetarian diet, as Muir had done, hoping that by doing this Muir "could teach me to become a nature listener. He describes valleys and rivers as musical instruments. . . . It was Muir who truly opened my ears to listening to nature as music."

As part of his cross-country recording trip, Hempton was especially eager to find Muir's stream—"walking the same ground as he did and listening to his cool mountain stream." That stream is outside Montgomery, Tennessee, in hilly terrain "offering scenic but discouraging valley views: almost every major valley has a road cutting through it." "The hills . . . echo traffic," Hempton writes, which could be a description of present-day Pennsylvania.

The search for Montgomery, even though he has it pinpointed on his topographical map, proves to be fruitless. Finally, he discovers a protected side valley with hollows and a little mountain stream, but the backcountry gravel road is filled with coal trucks. He waits until sunset, after the trucks hauling coal shut down, to start recording, but then a National Coal Corporation truck drives in, parks upstream, and starts sucking up the water, filling the "little valley with a piercing, mechanical whine."

Hempton learns from the driver that he takes four thousand gallons at a time from the stream in what has been labeled a Wildlife Management Area on the map, and makes twelve round-trip drives to the mine four miles away, working until 3:00 A.M., when another driver takes over. Not only does the water keep down road dust from the coal trucks, but it is used to refill the coal mine's pond. Hempton asks the driver if he knows where Montgomery is. The driver tells him he is standing in the town of Montgomery and next to Montgomery Creek.

So Hempton gives up his plan to record there. And as he nears Washington on the Chesapeake and Ohio towpath, where he walks the last hundred miles of his trip, he is appalled by the buildup of noise—trains, cars, trucks, but most of all continual air traffic all night long when he's camping out. Eventually, he meets with FAA officials, but they are particularly obdurate about not making any changes in flights over the Olympic National Park, and they continue to route passenger and military planes overhead.

I hope he is successful in his quixotic quest, but I'm certain he knows that Muir lost his fight to save the Hetch Hetchy Valley from the dam builders in 1913 and died the following year, worn out by his quest to preserve what he called the "other Yosemite," which became a reservoir for San Francisco.

We've watched for forty-four years as the remote home we bought in a mountain hollow has become noisier. It was never totally quiet. We are directly under a flight path from New York to California. Our son Steve, who was a frequent flyer in a previous job, says he could see our First Field from thirty thousand feet, but we rarely hear more than a low rumble. The military jets and helicopters, small private planes, and medical helicopters are much closer and louder. The family-owned limestone quarry in the valley below was bought up by a large conglomerate and has gone from barely noticeable to often cacophonous. And the small bypass at the base of our mountain transmogrified into Interstate 99. Sometimes on the loveliest days, it seems as if the traffic is coming over the mountain. Every neighbor has had a logging operation, with the accompanying whine of chainsaws and skidders. At the base of our mountain, since the 1850s, the major railroad line runs from New York to California. Recently, we've seen many more trains and tanker cars hauling fracked oil from the Dakotas and tar sands oil from Alberta.

Still, most of the time, we have no trouble hearing natural sounds above the din of modern life, and while I sympathize with Hempton's quest, I see an acceleration of human noise over the years ahead as humans "harvest" still more of the natural world to feed, clothe, and satisfy the desires of the increasing population.

Here on the Lake Trail, an ovenbird and red-eyed vireo sing, followed by a Baltimore oriole. A metalmark butterfly nectars on Philadelphia fleabane. We find the dried flower of a jack-in-the-pulpit. False Solomon's seal, the flower the late Lemont botanist George Beatty renamed more appropriately Solomon's plume, is still blooming. So too is sweet cicely. But by and large the spring wildflower extravaganza is over for the year.

And suddenly, as we near the end of the trail, it is quiet. It's 4:00 P.M. and the mower is finished for the day. We are too. But I can't help thinking that the Lake Trail is a misnomer. Except for glimpses at the wetland, Civil Engineering Camp, and spillway, we have little sense that we are circling a lake.

NOTE

1. This and the quotations in the following three paragraphs are from Gordon Hempton and John Grossmann, *One Square Inch of Silence: One Man's* *Search for Natural Silence in a Noisy World* (New York: Free Press, 2009), 244–45, 246, 249.

SITE 8

The Raptor Center

And so we have come full circle back to Shaver's Creek Environmental Center. Be sure to check out the exhibits inside the center—hands-on displays that teach about the constellations, soil types, and Pennsylvania mushrooms, the please-touch table with things like deer skulls and snake skins and bear fur, and the grip tester that compares the strength of your grip to the talons of a hawk or eagle. There are vivaria with wood turtles and red-eared sliders, good-sized black rat snakes, and even a fat timber rattler. But the real thrills are out back, in the raptor enclosures.

The ecoreflectors at the Raptor Center have been particularly fascinated, it seems, by the look in the eyes of the hawks, eagles, and owls kept here. The LTERPreters have gazed intently, trying to achieve intimacy, seeking a sense of connection, catching a glimpse of wildness, expressing their own love, awe, admiration, wonder. And the ecoreflectors have been gazed at in return, the eye contact unhindered by the bars of each bird's enclosure—which is a kind way of saying "cage."

The birds here have been brought to Shaver's Creek injured after being hit by bullets or cars, or zapped on power lines. They can't be released back into the wild, but they manage to bring a bit of wildness close to us. Of all the ecoreflection sites, this is the one where we can come in closest contact with wild creatures—and yet also the one where we are most conscious of the way human activity can affect wild things and can act as a constraint on wildness. These birds are behind bars, their movements restricted. It's a necessary imprisonment, of course, for the birds' own safety, and they are well cared for by diligent and well-trained interns. The bars might remind us of the ways in which human mediation has become necessary in order to help preserve the wild. And perhaps wildness has no better ambassa-dors than these birds, drawing fascinated visitors from nearby towns, giving them a startling glimpse into the power and mystery and grace of the more-than-human world. The birds in these cages are a meta-phor for the whole Stone Valley landscape—damaged at one time by human activity, now preserved by it as part of a managed ecosystem. That managed landscape, those birds—perhaps personal contact with them can be the means by which an ethic of care for the natural world can be sparked and nurtured.

Earning Intimacy at the Raptor Center

DAVID TAYLOR (2013)

It's early in the morning, and no one is here at the Raptor Center except me. The benches are wet from dew, but it's worth soggy shorts to sit and take in the amphitheater. The bald eagles are making their cackling squeak calls; it seems to me that they are calling to each other across their roomy cages as one waits for the other and then responds. Each has its cage to itself, but their cages are close, so they can easily see each other. I'm guessing they enjoy the company and conversation.

The naturalists told me that one of these eagles had a cage mate that died not long ago. As I'm listening to them, I can't help feeling a bit of sorrow, wondering if they are remembering their companion. I have this wonderful/dangerous tendency to filter through my emotions. As I tell folks, I cry at lots of things, low art, high art, and sadness or beauty wherever I imagine it: Tony Danza's *Angels in the Outfield*; Hank Williams's songs (I'm talking Sr., as Jr.'s best work just inspires people to throw whiskey bottles or watch football); well-sprayed graffiti; an act of compassion; the shape of light in the bottom of the Grand Canyon; lucky moments of inspiration. The risks are obvious: sentimentality, overreaction, ignorance about the actual object. The returns are equally obvious: love, connection, openness.

When my daughter was a little girl, she once asked Bob Pyle, one of the world's best lepidopterists, if butterflies feel. "Do you mean if they sense the world around them or if they have emotions?" he asked. "I don't know," she answered. Bob, having a big soul, smiled and paused. He then described a butterfly's central nervous system and the relative size of its brain matter, but concluded, "I don't know either."

How does one experience the world without emotion? I don't know. Nor should I want to. That's not to say I don't want to see the world as a naturalist, but I don't want to give up what I am, either.

It's important to see the world with some level of objectivity. I tell my students that they shouldn't write a poem about a flower they can't identify; it's creating a false intimacy with something or someone because they haven't earned a real one. Thus, while I'm not a good naturalist, I try to make sure and balance this tendency to emote by talking to good scientists and naturalists, reading the guidebooks, keeping good journals. I'm still at this place where these are distinct approaches, though, not a seamless response.

I've read the signs outside the cages about the natural history and habits of bald eagles. I've also read about their decimation by loss of habitat and prey, through being hunted as nuisances, and by the impact of DDT. Once down to only a few hundred nesting pairs, bald eagles have been brought back through law, protection, and habitat preservation, and perhaps most important, through folks' sentiment for the bald eagle as our nation's symbol. Caring is probably what motivated us most.

By now, a few adults are wandering through the Raptor Center, drinking coffee or smoking a cigarette before their leadership workshop starts on the other side of the Environmental Center. We nod at each other but don't want to talk because we are focused on the eagles. We're reading the signs and learning about them, but we're also looking through the fences and listening intently, enough to still us beyond cursory greetings. We can't help feeling something, standing by these eagle cages, seeing the birds' keen eyes on us this cool, wet morning, imagining whether their calls spark for them a memory of taking prey, a reminiscence of pairing, a muscle twitch of riding thermals. We're trying to earn an intimacy worthy of telling others this story.

Eagle Acquaintances

HANNAH INGLESBY (2014)

In the bald eagle enclosure, I feel incongruous: here are my heavy bones so near this creature of speed and flight. Though I've been told not to make eye contact, it's hard not to stare at its white crown. I feel a little starstruck. This is the emblem of our country! Its razor-hooked beak is so yellow . . . and big. The bald eagle vocalizes in warning, a funny sound that I'd not expect to come from this bird, a sound that reminds me of a cross between a dolphin and a squirrel.

Each environmental education intern is assigned at least one week to work with the Raptor Center. On my first day in this role, I entered the bald eagle's enclosure alone, bucket in hand. Every day someone tidies the enclosures, using tongs to peel strings of guts from stumps, picking up sticky down feathers, and raking the gravel clean. I had told myself I wouldn't be intimidated by the eagle. But as he postured, dodging toward rather than away from me, I couldn't keep my heart from beating fast. This bird is meant for power. While I am not a rabbit, I still eyed its talons with fear-tinged awe. Nothing bad came to pass that day, and a few days ago, as I again picked up the bald eagle's feathers, my heart beat slower. The eagle quieted as I hummed.

I feel out of place, and honored, in all the enclosures. While I've not spent a lot of time with the birds this summer, I do consider them fond acquaintances. They are all quirky, majestic, and, were they not permanently disabled, remarkable hunters. Though I know they were—and are—wild, it's hard for me not to anthropomorphize them. The barred owls look perpetually perplexed, as if they've just woken from a nap. The kestrel flies, trilling, to the wires of her enclosure, looking for a treat. The black vulture with its ruffed hood reminds me of a Jim Henson creation. The turkey vulture tries to untie my shoes. And the barn owls hiss and bob and spread their wings grumpily from their high perch when I enter. The screech owls remind me of little old men.

All day long, off and on, the golden eagle squawks. During one week as a camp counselor, I had a camper who loved to imitate her noise. I wonder what she thought when this wisp of a boy would stand in front of her, responding to her high-pitched calls.

As I stroll through the Raptor Center today, a season of images drift through my thoughts. I recall the pungency of dead rat as it's snipped in half with shears. There's the way a toad eats, waiting in front of a mealworm, motionless, then flicking out a pink tongue and, as it swallows, its protuberant eyes closing and sinking into its head. I think of how the rat snake feels to hold: muscled, heavier than I'd expect, cool, its scales sometimes catching on my fingernails. I think back on the festivals at which the Raptor Center tabled. Sometimes I'd sit in front of a display of wings and feathers, explaining how the fringed edge of an owl wing helps it fly silently. I'd talk to people as I held up animal pelts or explained the differences between venomous and nonvenomous snakes. There was the guy who told me about eating roast snapping turtle, and the stories of a family who would watch coyotes play in their backyard.

The Raptor Center is, for me, about the intersection of people and wildlife. My continued feeling of incongruousness as I encounter the animals here is evidence of my awe. The sight, the flight, the radical ability to survive with only the tools of their own bodies—I am humbled by these animals and grateful for the rare close look at them that the Raptor Center provides.

The Raptor (Eye) Center

JULIANNE LUTZ WARREN (OCTOBER 2015)

During her three-month performance "The Artist Is Present," Marina Abramović spent all day, every day, sitting in a chair, exchanging looks with museum visitors seated across from her. Person by person, barely looking at any other part of each singular body, Abramović shared mutual, often extended gazes with a total of 1,565 pairs of eyes. Many times, people became emotional, weeping during this intimate experience. Seeing themselves being seen in her tended to unleash participants' vulnerability, Abramović explained. And she felt herself revealed in the mirroring of others; they changed her, too. "I know them," she said in a 2010 interview for MOMA's *Inside/Out*—each sitter, "they're like family."[1]

Birds and humans don't usually get so close or stay still long enough to stare. As a visitor in the Raptor Center, I did my best, in a few hours accumulated during the course of my stay, to exchange looks with a mere thirty pairs of avian eyes. The birds had not volunteered for this, and not all of them responded to my advances by returning glances. This certainly was each one's prerogative. In such cases, I stepped back. Some did agree, though, if just for a moment. Intellectually, I knew that not only each species, but each individual, was unique. I also understood the scientific evidence supporting human kinship with birds, and with all life. In this eyeballing practice, though, I *felt* the particularity of each one, and, yes, also, for better or worse, the fact that they're like family.

Among the most haunting eyes were the short-eared owl's—with shadowy lids and *wide* black pupils rimmed in stunning gold. It was not only their beauty but their intent that got me. On our first quick encounter, just before noon on that cold rainy day of my arrival, this bird's stare felt both unshrinking and uncertain. Perhaps he was evaluating my charm. What I saw mirrored in his eyes, I recognized, were my own exertions to perform self-confidence. Two days later, in the early frozen morning, his look felt equally direct, but with a gain in dubiousness. As I drew close, he hissed at me from his perch without moving away. My gaze this time alarmed him. What had I reflected that he felt, and how had I fallen short? At about 1:45 on the warm afternoon of the twenty-second, I returned for feeding time. Intern Emily Anne Moore and volunteer Samantha Goebel generously invited me to follow them around. As the three of us descended, the short-eared owl, as if staring into space, seemed to ignore us and the three mice that Samantha placed with tongs into his food box. The traits that the bird's bearing brought to mind included awareness, firmness, and self-determination. If accurate, I suspect that these qualities did not come to him any more easily than they do to humans living in wing-torn captivity.

Indeed, birds and hominids are bound in a legacy as creations of earth. Three hundred and ten million years ago, both of our lines, in a sense, occupied a common, fertile egg. Then we branched off, as siblings will, into our own odysseys. Scientifically speaking, our respective ancestors probably continued developing on different fragments of the rifted landmass of Gondwana. Raptors developed millions of years ago, diversified and dispersed among continents. Arriving in Africa, avian sorts reunited with the still-developing humans who became our type a mere two hundred thousand years ago, then scattered quickly. Until, eventually, in all our many still-unfurling forms, birds and humans intertwined across the whole world.

When our lineage diverged, those long ages ago, birds and mammals carried forward to their progenies the same basic design of water-based eyes, which continued evolving. Most human retinas now have cones for receiving a spectrum of red, green, and blue. Birds not only have more of these cones; they also have cones for ultraviolet, plus colored oil droplets. So most avian eyes can see multihued rainbows, and shades of feathers, hard for people to imagine. Each heritage of brains also developed in different ways. Recently, scientists have discerned that "birdbrained" does not mean smallminded. In fact, birds and mammals, including raptors and humans, share capacities for complex cognitive behaviors, such as remembering, learning, and communicating, including exchanges of empathy along with arrays of feelings.

In any case, beyond science, you know it when you see it:

In the kestrel's glossy brown eyes, so near my face, I recognized a ferocity of need, tenderizing, which drew me close.

The directness of the peregrine's dark look reflected my own unrepentant wildness.

The turkey vulture's smaller eyes were, to me, alert yet inscrutable. Perhaps I must spend more time with carrion.

The bald eagles—one pair, male, yellowed with age, the younger females black—kept their distance, as did I, while the elder's voice, though kind of funny-sounding, found its way right through me—as the peregrine up the hill joined in, wailing, and then a crow called, free-flying overhead.

The golden eagle turned away her back, and her gaze. I was heartbroken.

All kinds of birds may get to know us, too, as individuals. The black vulture, with impish affection, had eyes only for Torri Withrow, an environmental education intern, who replied, "I could sit in here all day."

That sounded like a very good idea.

NOTE

1. Marina Abramović, "Marina Abramović: The Artist Speaks," interview by Daniela Stigh and Zoë Jackson, *Inside/Out* (blog), Museum of Modern Art, New York, June 3, 2010, http://www.moma.org/explore /inside_out/2010/06/03/marina -abramovic-the-artist-speaks/.

I Remember a Bird

KATIE FALLON (2016)

I remember a bird: a red-shouldered hawk, scooped from a ridgetop pasture in West Virginia. Bleeding. The end of her wing an angry wound, a nub, coagulating and swollen. I remember closing my fingers around her scaly, pale yellow legs, holding her hooked head, while my husband, Jesse, examined the wing. I remember the way her heart drummed within her speckled breast. I remember her long barred tail, each feather impeccable still, despite her being grounded. Grounded, forever.

Radiographs revealed a dusting of lead in the wound: gunshot. A federal offense, now, but that doesn't always matter to someone alone in a field with a rifle. I don't understand what motivates someone to shoot a hawk. Probably a deadly mix of cruelty and boredom, although "chickens" is the answer more likely given. In "Hurt Hawks," the poet Robinson Jeffers famously wrote, "I'd sooner, except the penalties, kill a man than a hawk."[1] I can relate.

Working in wildlife rehabilitation is heartbreaking. But we do it anyway. Perhaps because of guilt or obligation or love or kinship. We could have—should have?—killed that hawk. Eased her out of this life gently, first inducing sleep and then giving the injection to quiet her wild heart, reducing her to limp feathers, slack talons. But we didn't. Using a wooden tongue depressor, Jesse spread a glob of gooey salve on the hawk's wound and then bandaged it carefully, slowly, while his brows ran together. For weeks we nursed the wound, changed the bandage, medicated, fattened her on dead mice. Watched the wild eyes watch us.

More than ten years have passed since I first met that red-shouldered hawk, and now I see her again. I'm sitting on a sun-warmed bench in the back row of the outdoor amphitheater at Shaver's Creek Environmental Center. It's September. A warm breeze tumbles fallen maple leaves; they rustle like the pages of a book. Enclosures on the amphitheater's perimeter hold birds of prey: eagles, hawks, owls, vultures. Across from me is the red-shoulder. She grips a turf-wrapped perch with one foot and tucks the other beneath her. She cocks her head to watch the pine trees that surround us. Her wings, black and brown flecked with white, with red splashed across the shoulders, are folded comfortably over her back. Her long tail hangs straight down. She appears relaxed; I'm glad, relieved. A decade ago, we'd reached out to Shaver's Creek and asked if they had space to provide a permanent home for our damaged hawk. We had made the three-hour drive from West Virginia, bird tucked inside a dark cardboard box. And she's still here, today, sharing an enclosure with a short-eared owl, enjoying the September sunshine.

A small boy, perhaps four years old, rounds a corner and approaches the hawk. He reaches up and grabs the interpretive sign in front of her enclosure, pulling himself higher. The hawk turns her head to watch him. An older man, his grandfather, I imagine, walks behind him and reads the sign. The boy leans back, looks up, and locks eyes with the hawk, a creature from another world, a piece of wild woods and sky. The universe holds its breath. The boy releases the sign and looks away. He picks up a stick and hops down the path and around a bend, with grandfather strolling behind.

The universe resumes, exhales, begins to roll again. I exhale too, and realize that I've just witnessed a change, a different future now unfolding. How much different it will be—who can know? But I am certain: whatever universe would have unfolded *without* that moment between hawk, boy, grandfather, and September day: we will never know it.

A hundred years from now, what will that boy have done? Cradled another hurt hawk, perhaps, plucked bloody from a pasture or from a roadside, stunned? Maybe he will simply notice hawks, notice birds, look skyward more often than he would have in a different future. Maybe his capacity for empathy increased. This hawk changed me, too, and changed Jesse, who is now a veterinarian, caring for hawks daily. And here I am, recording my reflections at Shaver's Creek, having written two books about birds and ecosystems and still in love with the world. My hawk-inspired words are free and wild, and hopefully they'll keep flying even after I'm gone, after boy and grandfather, after hawk.

Across the amphitheater, she wags her barred tail, looks up, then looks at me. No, she looks past me, above me, at something in the sky, something soaring.

NOTE

1. Robinson Jeffers, *Selected Poems* (New
York: Vintage Books, 1965), 45.

BIBLIOGRAPHY

Abramović, Marina. "Marina Abramović: The Artist Speaks." Interview by Daniela Stigh and Zoë Jackson. *Inside/Out* (blog), Museum of Modern Art, New York, June 3, 2010. http://www.moma.org/explore/inside _out/2010/06/03/marina-abramovic-the-artist-speaks/.

Africa, J. Simpson. *History of Huntingdon and Blair Counties, Pennsylvania*. Philadelphia: Louis H. Everts, 1883. Reprint, Evansville, Ind.: Unigraphic, 1977.

Barnes, John H., and W. D. Sevon. *Geological Story of Pennsylvania*. 3rd ed. Harrisburg: Pennsylvania Department of Conservation and Natural Resources, 2002.

Cox, Thomas R. *The Lumberman's Frontier: Three Centuries of Land Use, Society, and Change in America's Forests*. Corvallis: Oregon State University Press, 2010.

Csikszentmihalyi, Mihaly. *Flow: The Psychology of Optimal Experience*. New York: Harper Perennial, 2008.

Eiseley, Loren. "The Flow of the River." In *The Immense Journey: An Imaginative Naturalist Explores the Mysteries of Man and Nature*, 15–28. New York: Vintage Books, 1959.

Eliot, T. S. "The Hollow Men." All Poetry. https://allpoetry.com/The-Hollow-Men.

Emerson, Ralph Waldo. "Circles." Bartleby.com. http://www.bartleby .com/5/109.html.

Foster, David R., ed. *Hemlock: A Forest Giant on the Edge*. New Haven: Yale University Press, 2014.

Frost, Robert. "Education by Poetry." In *Selected Prose of Robert Frost*, edited by Hyde Cox and Edward Connery Lathem, 33–46. New York: Holt, Rinehart and Winston, 1966.

———. *The Poetry of Robert Frost: The Collected Poems, Complete and Unabridged*. Edited by Edward Connery Lathem. New York: Henry Holt, 1969.

Goodrich, Charles. "Entries into the Forest." In *Forest Under Story: Creative Inquiry in an Old-Growth Forest*, edited by Nathaniel Brodie, Charles Goodrich, and Frederick J. Swanson, 5–14. Seattle: University of Washington Press, 2016.

Goodrich, Charles, and Frederick J. Swanson. "Long-Term Ecological Reflections: Art Among Science Among Place." *Terrain.org: A Journal of the Built + Natural Environments*, August 28, 2016. http://www .terrain.org/2016/guest-editorial/long-term-ecological-reflections/.

Harned, Joseph E. *Wild Flowers of the Alleghanies*. Oakland, Md.: Joseph E. Harned, 1931.

Hempton, Gordon, and John Grossmann. *One Square Inch of Silence: One Man's Search for Natural Silence in a Noisy World*. New York: Free Press, 2009.

Herzog, Werner. *Conquest of the Useless: Reflections from the Making of "Fitzcarraldo."* Translated by Krishna Winston. New York: Ecco, 2010.

Hess, Scott. "Imagining an Everyday Nature." *Interdisciplinary Studies in Literature and Environment* 17, no. 1 (2010): 85–112.

H. J. Andrews Experimental Forest. "Forest Log: An On-line Journal of Poems, Essays, Articles, and Other Creative Reflections on the Forest." http:// www.andrewsforestlog.org/category/writing.

Jeffers, Robinson. *Selected Poems*. New York: Vintage Books, 1965.

Kawamoto, Koji. *The Poetics of Japanese Verse: Poetics, Structure, Meter*. Translated by Stephen Collington, Kevin Collins, and Gustav Heldt. Tokyo: University of Tokyo Press, 2000.

Kline, Benjamin F. G., Jr. *"Pitch Pine and Prop Timber": The Logging Railroads of South-Central Pennsylvania*. Strasburg, Pa.: Railroad Museum of Pennsylvania, 1999.

Longfellow, Henry Wadsworth. "The Village Blacksmith." *Longfellow: Searchable Database of Longfellow Poems*. http://www.hwlongfellow .org/poems_poem.php?pid=38.

Lutz, Lara. "Tiny Insect Toppling Region's Majestic Hemlocks." *Bay Journal*, June 9, 2015. http://www.bayjournal.com/article/tiny_insect_top pling_regions_majestic_hemlocks.

Magrane, Eric, and Chris Cokinos, eds. *The Sonoran Desert: A Literary Field Guide*. Tucson: University of Arizona Press, 2016.

Mann, Charles C. *1491: New Revelations of the Americas Before Columbus*. New York: Vintage Books, 2006.

Marshall, Ian. "Winter Tracings and Transcendental Leaps: Henry Thoreau's Skating." *Papers on Language and Literature* 29, no. 4 (1993): 459–74.

Marshall-McKelvey, Jacy. "The History of Shaver's Creek." Unpublished manuscript. Shaver's Creek Environmental Center, 2012.

McKibben, Bill. *The End of Nature*. New York: Random House, 1999.

Muir, John. *John of the Mountains: The Unpublished Journals of John Muir*. 1938. Edited by Linnie Marsh Wolfe. Madison: University of Wisconsin Press, 1979.

———. *A Thousand-Mile Walk to the Gulf*. 1916. New York: Mariner Books, 1998.

Newcomb, Lawrence. *Newcomb's Wildflower Guide*. Boston: Little, Brown, 1989.

Peterson, Roger Tory, and Margaret McKenny. *A Field Guide to Wildflowers of Northeastern and North-Central North America*. Peterson Field Guide Series. New York: Houghton Mifflin Harcourt, 1998.

Prieto, Eric. "Geocriticism Meets Ecocriticism: Bertrand Westphal and Environmental Thinking." In *Ecocriticism and Geocriticism: Overlapping Territories in Environmental and Spatial Literary Studies*, edited by Robert T. Tally Jr. and Christine M. Battista, 19–35. New York: Palgrave, 2016.

Primack, Richard. *Walden Warming: Climate Change Comes to Thoreau's Woods*. Chicago: University of Chicago Press, 2014.

Rawson, Hugh, and Margaret Miner, eds. *The Oxford Dictionary of American Quotations*. 2nd ed. New York: Oxford University Press, 2006.

Sandburg, Carl. "Fog." Poetry Foundation. http://www.poetryfoundation.org/poems-and-poets/poems/detail/45032.

Shedd, Nancy S. *Huntingdon County, Pennsylvania: An Inventory of Historic Engineering and Industrial Sites*. Washington, D.C.: U.S. Department of the Interior, National Park Service, 1991.

Stevenson, Donald D., H. Arthur Meyer, and Ronald A. Bartoo. *Management Plan for Stone Valley Experimental Forest*. University Park: Pennsylvania State University, 1943.

Tallmadge, John. *Meeting the Tree of Life: A Teacher's Path*. Salt Lake City: University of Utah Press, 1997.

Thoreau, Henry David. *Walden*. Edited by J. Lyndon Shanley. Princeton: Princeton University Press, 2004.

———. "A Winter Walk." In *Excursions*, edited by Joseph J. Moldenhauer, 48–67. Princeton: Princeton University Press, 2007.

Westphal, Bertrand. Foreword. In *Geocritical Explorations: Space, Place, and Mapping in Literary and Cultural Studies*, edited by Robert T. Tally Jr., ix–xvi. New York: Palgrave, 2011.

Yeats, William Butler. "The Second Coming." Poetry Foundation. https://www.poetryfoundation.org/poems/43290/the-second-coming.

ABOUT THE CONTRIBUTORS

One of central Pennsylvania's local treasures, naturalist and writer **Marcia Bonta** is the author of more than three hundred magazine articles, including her monthly column The Naturalist's Eye, which she has written for the *Pennsylvania Game News* for twenty-three years. She has also written nine books—among them *Escape to the Mountain*, an account of her family's move to Brush Mountain in the 1970s, *Women in the Field: America's Pioneering Women Naturalists*, and her four "Appalachian seasons" books: *Appalachian Spring, Appalachian Summer, Appalachian Autumn*, and *Appalachian Winter*.

A prominent literary ecocritic as well as a nature writer, **Michael P. Branch** is professor of literature and environment at the University of Nevada, Reno. He is a co-founder and past president of the Association for the Study of Literature and Environment, and he has published eight books and more than two hundred articles, essays, and reviews. His creative nonfiction includes pieces that have received honorable mention for the Pushcart Prize and been recognized as "notable essays" in *The Best American Essays* (three times), *The Best American Science and Nature Writing*, and *The Best American Nonrequired Reading* (a humor anthology). His creative work has appeared in the *Utne Reader, Orion, Slate, Ecotone, Places, Whole Terrain, Red Rock Review*, and other magazines and journals. Mike's most recent books are *Raising Wild: Dispatches from a Home in the Wilderness; Rants from the Hill: On Packrats, Bobcats, Wildfires, Curmudgeons, a Drunken Mary Kay Lady, and Other Encounters with the Wild in the High Desert*; and *"The Best Read Naturalist": Nature Writings of Ralph Waldo Emerson* (co-edited with Clinton Mohs). Mike lives with his wife and two young daughters in the remote, high-elevation Great Basin Desert of western Nevada.

Todd Davis is the author of five full-length collections of poetry—*Winterkill, In the Kingdom of the Ditch, The Least of These, Some Heaven*, and *Ripe*—and a limited-edition chapbook, *Household of Water, Moon, and Snow: The Thoreau Poems*. He edited the nonfiction collection *Fast Break to Line Break: Poets on the Art of Basketball*, and co-edited the anthology *Making Poems*. His writing has been featured on Garrison Keillor's radio program *The Writer's Almanac* and in Ted Kooser's syndicated newspaper column American Life in Poetry. His poems have won the Gwendolyn Brooks Poetry Prize, the Chautauqua Editors Prize, and the *Foreword Reviews* Book of the Year Bronze Award, and have been nominated several times for the Pushcart Prize. His poetry has been published in such noted journals and magazines as *American Poetry Review, Iowa Review, North American Review, Missouri Review, Gettysburg Review, Orion, West Branch,* and *Poetry Daily.* He is a fellow at the Black Earth Institute and teaches environmental studies, creative writing, and American literature at Pennsylvania State University's Altoona College.

A lifelong resident of Appalachia, **Katie Fallon** is the author of *Vulture: The Private Life of an Unloved Bird* and *Cerulean Blues: A Personal Search for a Vanishing Songbird,* which was a finalist for the Reed Environmental Writing Award for outstanding writing on the southern landscape. She has also co-written, with Bill Wilson, a children's book, *Look, See the Bird!* Katie's essays have appeared in a variety of literary journals and magazines, including *Fourth Genre, River Teeth, Ecotone, Appalachian Heritage, Isotope, Fourth River,* and *the minnesota review.* Katie is one of the founders of the Avian Conservation Center of Appalachia, a nonprofit organization dedicated to conserving wild birds through scientific research, outreach and public education, and rescue and rehabilitation. Not surprisingly, her first word was "bird." Katie's great-great grandfather, great-grandfather, and grandfather were coal miners in West Virginia and Pennsylvania. Both of her parents were public school teachers. Katie lives in Cheat Neck, West Virginia, and has taught creative writing at Virginia Tech and West Virginia University.

David Gessner is the author of nine books, including *Sick of Nature, My Green Manifesto,* and *The Tarball Chronicles,* which won the 2012 Reed Environmental Writing Award and the Association for the Study of Literature and Environment's Creative Writing Award in 2011 and 2012. His *Return of the Osprey* was chosen by the Boston Globe as one of the top ten nonfiction books of the year and by the Book of the Month Club as one of its top books of the year. He also puts a lot of energy into blogging in his Wild Life column with the Natural Resources Defense Council, and Bill and Dave's Cocktail Hour, a website he created with the writer Bill Roorbach. He still dreams of winning the national championship in ultimate Frisbee but knows it will never happen.

A central Pennsylvania native, **Hannah Inglesby** attended Warren Wilson College in Swannanoa, North Carolina, earning a BA in environmental studies in 2010. She served in AmeriCorps for two years near Philadelphia and then worked for the social service agency the Arc of Centre County. In the summer of 2014 she was an environmental education intern at Shaver's Creek Environmental Center. Since then, she has enjoyed working at Fox

Hill Gardens, where she is a nursery worker and landscaper, the State College
Friends School, where she is an assistant teacher, and Lila Yoga Studios.

John Lane is professor of environmental studies at Wofford College and
director of the college's Goodall Environmental Studies Center. The author
of a dozen books of poetry and prose, Lane published his first novel, *Fate
Moreland's Widow*, with Pat Conroy's Story River Books at the University of
South Carolina Press in 2015. Lane's latest books of poems are *The Old Rob
Poems* and *Abandoned Quarry: New and Selected Poems*. Among his works
of nature writing are *Waist Deep in Black Water*, *Chattooga*, *Circling Home*,
and *My Paddle to the Sea*. Lane has won numerous awards, including the
2001 Reed Environmental Writing Award from the Southern Environmental
Law Center. In 2011 he won the Glenna Luschei Prairie Schooner Award,
and in 2012 *Abandoned Quarry* was named the SIBA (Southern Independent
Booksellers Alliance) Poetry Book of the Year. He was inducted into the South
Carolina Academy of Authors in 2014. Along with his wife, Betsy Teter, he is
one of the co-founders of the Hub City Writers Project.

Carolyn Mahan is a professor of biology and environmental studies at Penn
State Altoona. Her research interests include the study of biodiversity in
threatened ecosystems, the effects of human-modified landscapes on wildlife,
and the behavioral ecology of sciurids. In addition to her scholarly research,
she has served as a consultant to the National Park Service, conducting natural
resource assessments for several national parks in the eastern United States.

A professor of English and environmental studies at Penn State Altoona, **Ian
Marshall** is a past president of the Association for the Study of Literature
and Environment. He is the author of four books of literary ecocriticism:
Story Line: Exploring the Literature of the Appalachian Trail; *Peak Experiences:
Walking Meditations on Literature, Nature, and Need*; *Walden by Haiku*; and
*Border Crossings: Walking the Haiku Path on the International Appalachian
Trail*.

While being homeschooled growing up in State College, **Jacy Marshall-
McKelvey** worked for five years as a volunteer at the Raptor Center at Shaver's
Creek Environmental Center. He went on to graduate with a degree in geography from Penn State University and is the author of *The History of Shaver's
Creek*, forthcoming online (on the Shaver's Creek Environmental Center website) and in book form. He is also the author of *Centre County*, an unpublished
historical novel about the area.

Steven Rubin is an associate professor of art in the photography program at
Penn State University. Before taking that post, he worked around the world for

more than twenty years as a photojournalist and documentary photographer. A 2013 Fulbright-Nehru Scholar in northeast India, he was also a Nieman Fellow at Harvard, an Alicia Patterson Journalism Fellow, and a Community Fellow and Media Fellow with the Open Society Institute. His current projects investigate the rise of wind energy in Kansas, the precarious conditions of Burmese Chin refugees in Mizoram, India, and the social and environmental impacts of Marcellus Shale gas development in Pennsylvania.

David Taylor is an assistant professor of sustainability in the Sustainability Studies Program at Stony Brook University. His creative writing and research cross disciplinary boundaries and genres—poetry, creative nonfiction, scholarship, and science/technical writing. He is the author of a collection of poetry, *Praying up the Sun*, and a work of creative nonfiction, *The Lawson's Fork: Headwaters to the Confluence*. David is also the editor of *South Carolina Naturalists: An Anthology, 1700–1860*, and *Pride of Place: A Contemporary Anthology of Texas Nature Writing*. In October 2008 he led a group of eight students on a forty-mile trip down the Brazos River, reenacting John Graves's trip fifty years ago.

Julianne Lutz Warren is the author of *Aldo Leopold's Odyssey*, an intellectual biography tracing the famous twentieth-century ecologist's ethical notion of "land health." Warren holds a master of arts in linguistics, a master of science in wildlife ecology, and a PhD in conservation biology, all from the University of Illinois. A relative of early twentieth-century nature writer John Burroughs and a former president of Woodchuck Lodge, in Roxbury, New York, Warren taught environmental studies at New York University, where she received the 2013 Martin Luther King, Jr. Faculty Award for her work with students on climate justice. Her current scholarly and creative work explores authentic hope in the Anthropocene, including what may be learned from listening to the echoes of extinct birdsong. She serves as a Fellow of the Center for Humans and Nature.

Author and naturalist **Scott Weidensaul** has written more than two dozen books on natural history, including *Living on the Wind: Across the Hemisphere with Migratory Birds*, a Pulitzer Prize finalist; *The Ghost with Trembling Wings*, about the search for species that may or may not be extinct; and *Of a Feather: A Brief History of American Birding*. Weidensaul lectures widely on wildlife and environmental topics and is an active field researcher, specializing in birds of prey and hummingbirds. He lives in the Appalachians of eastern Pennsylvania, the heart of the old colonial frontier.